Page 261

Page 279

Page 297

Page 313

Page 321

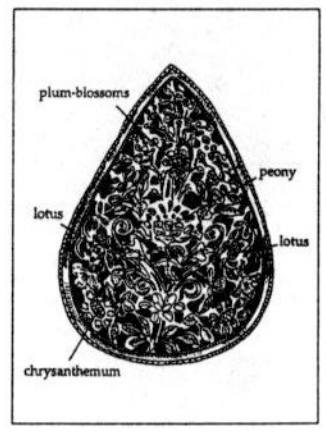

Page 329

Contents

Editor
Dr. Valerie Steele
The Museum at the Fashion Institute of Technology, E201
Seventh Avenue at 27th Street
New York, NY 10001-5992
USA

Fax +1 212 924 3958
e-mail: steelemajor@earthlink.net

BERG

Fashion Theory, Volume 1, Issue 3, pp.245–246
Reprints available directly from the Publishers.

© Roxanne Lowit

Letter from the Editor

Fashion Theory has received a lot of press coverage, in newspapers ranging from *The Guardian* and *Die Zeit* to fashion magazines such as *Elle* and *Harper's Bazaar*. The journalists at *Artforum* and *Time Out* were a little sarcastic about the possibility that professors might know anything about fashion. But Robin Givhan at *The Washington Post* thought that a "brainy" approach to fashion was great, and *W* even suggested that fashionistas who saw themselves as intellectuals might trade in their Comme des Garçons for subscriptions to *Fashion Theory*.

It is true that academic discourse can be at least as opaque as "Voguespeak," and some of the articles in *Fashion Theory* have proved difficult for readers unaccustomed to the vocabulary. The fact that this magazine has an extremely heterogeneous readership makes it inevitable that we can not always communicate perfectly with each other, but it is my hope that both writers and readers will persist in the attempt. Certainly, the response to *Fashion Theory* has been extremely gratifying, and demonstrates how many people believe fashion is important enough to take seriously. I'm also delighted that the magazine has attracted readers from around the world. We've had terrific launch parties at The Courtauld in London and the Fashion Institute of Technology in New York, but I have to confess that I'm most looking forward to launching the magazine in Florence this June under the auspices of Pitti Immagine.

In addition to my own presentation about the magazine, there will be brief talks by two contributors to *Fashion Theory*: The Metropolitan Museum of Art's costume curator, Richard Martin, and my colleague at The Museum at FIT, Laird Borrelli.

In this issue of *Fashion Theory*, Laird Borrelli undertakes an historical and semiotic analysis of "Voguespeak." Her fascinating essay demonstrates that the language of fashion changes over time, just as the fashions themselves do. Fashion magazines have their own unique jargon. Back in the 1950s the language was hortatory. The top magazines, such as *Vogue* and *Harper's Bazaar*, adopted a quasi-religious tone, as though each and every fashion trend had been determined on high, and the votaries of fashion must follow suit or risk being cast into the outer darkness. When fashion editors proclaimed "Think pink!" readers were expected to obey immediately. Middle-level magazines, such as *Mademoiselle* and *Glamour*, directed towards a younger and less sophisticated audience, also made authoritative pronouncements, but combined them with a cajoling tone: "Pink is in! Try it! You'll like it!"

The content of fashion magazines changed dramatically in the 1960s, but editorial authority remained undiminished. It may even have increased, as confused middle aged readers struggled to understand successive fashion revolutions. It was only in the 1970s that readers began to rebel, forcing editors onto the defensive. As a result, they tended to waffle: Long skirts might be in, but short ones were nice, too, and so were trousers. Freedom of choice became fashion's new mantra. Within a few years, however, the arbiters of fashion were again dispensing wisdom, although they took care never to sound really dictatorial. As Borrelli demonstrates, *Vogue*'s most famous fashion editor, Diana Vreeland, spoke a very different language from her successors, Grace Mirabella and Anna Wintour. Fluency in the latest fashion terminology is clearly essential for industry professionals, but at least minimal comprehension is also desirable for the common reader if s/he is to make any sense at all of the text in fashion magazines. It is certainly not immediately apparent what is meant by such expressions as "real clothes" or "a more relaxed look."

Speaking of relaxed, the next issue of *Fashion Theory* will be devoted to the subject of "Hair." After that, the first three issues of 1998 will cover the usual eclectic range of fashion-related topics, to be followed by another special thematic issue, possibly on ethnic identity.

Although most of our articles have dealt with twentieth-century fashion, potential contributors are reminded that we are also interested in articles on fashion in previous centuries.

Sincerely yours,

Valerie Steele

Fashion Theory, Volume 1, Issue 3, pp.247–260
Reprints available directly from the Publishers.
Photocopying permitted by licence only.

Dressing Up and Talking about It: Fashion Writing in *Vogue* from 1968 to 1993

Laird O'Shea Borrelli

Laird Borrelli is a Phi Beta Kappa graduate of Boston College with a BA in English Literature. She holds an MA in Museum Studies/Costume History from the Fashion Institute of Technology and is currently employed as a curatorial assistant at the Museum at FIT's Costume Collection.

Where would fashion be without literature?
Diana Vreeland, *D.V.*

Moreover, isn't Fashion a literature?
Roland Barthes, *The Fashion System*

Introduction

The subject of fashion writing is Fashion. Fashion itself is a glorious and protean fiction. The creation of a "glossy" like *Vogue* is not unlike

the creation of a work of literature. Both magazine editors and authors craft their own worlds. Fashion fictions in *Vogue* are communicated using images and words.

Much attention has been given to fashion images—both advertising and editorial—by art and fashion historians, sociologists, analysts of the media, and feminists. All acknowledge the potency of the fashion image, but their conclusions have often been negative, focusing on the (fashion) media's (stereotypical) portrayal of women. What is understood is that the layout, illustrations, and photographs of a magazine like *Vogue* successfully communicate (fashion) information colorfully, strikingly, quickly, to millions of women (Ballaster et al. 1991, 36).[1] Some images, like that of the gun-slinging Verushka in a Saint Laurent safari top, become iconic.[2] Others, like Guy Bourdin's for Charles Jourdan, or more recently Steven Meisel's photographs for Calvin Klein, scandalize.

The seduction by the fashion image is immediate ("at first sight"), whereas the texts of fashion must be read word-for-word. Both image and word function to articulate fashion and to create its narratives. It is not surprising in our modern "Age of the Face" (Harris 1993, 134) that attention to the fashion image has been ascendant and fashion writing has been relegated to the role of accompanist. This can be attributed to the overall predominance of the image (especially through the electronic media) in our culture and also to the complicated relationship between what Roland Barthes has termed "image-clothing" and the "written garment" in fashion magazines (Barthes 1990, 3). Feminist studies of women's magazines have tended to concentrate on "women's service magazines" like *Good Housekeeping* rather than on "glossies" like *Vogue*.[3] The glossies have received attention from art historians who have focused on the work of fashion illustrators and photographers, but little attention has been paid to fashion writing.

Words and images behave in different ways. A picture of a miniskirt performs a different function than the naming of it. Barthes suggests that words make the image "*intelligible*: [that] it is not the object but the name that creates desire" (Barthes 1990, xii). The importance of language to fashion has been greatly "glossed" over by image-clothing. I assert, however, that fashion is perpetuated by the fictions constructed around it. Further, its evolution is dependent on the durability of its oral culture[4] (both written and voiced). Orality implies community. Not only do we dress up; we talk about it.

Just as fashion images have received more attention than fashion writing, so have the personalities of *Vogue* editors received more attention than their written editorial achievements. *Vogue* had three editors-in-chief between 1968 and 1993. Diana Vreeland, Grace Mirabella, and Anna Wintour have each produced very different fashion narratives. Their individual inflections relate not only to the environments (historical and sartorial) in which they worked but to

their different answers to the question: "What is Fashion?" In creating a semiology of fashion, Barthes described its language, on the whole, as being "institutional" (Barthes 1990, 186). My interest, however, is in the manner in which Vreeland, Mirabella, and Wintour have constructed individual voices from this institutional language.

I have chosen as my primary source the section of the magazine entitled "Vogue's Point of View"[5] and have limited my study to the Fall/Winter collection issues—a total of thirty-one issues between 1968 and 1993. By limiting my study to September issues (the fashion year's most important) I was able to cover twenty-five years of fashion and three editorships. Six Vreeland, nineteen Mirabella, and six Wintour issues are reviewed.

Point of View was chosen as a primary source for several reasons, not the least of which is that it has appeared in every September issue for twenty-five years. Its importance is suggested by its location: directly before the spreads that are the "heart" of the magazine (though not its "bread and butter"). Point of View exists to summarize, highlight, describe, promote, report, and instruct on the best of the new looks that appear in the fashion spreads. While the fashion spreads contain desirable images, fashion don'ts are incorporated into the text of Point of View. Sometimes they are gently stated: "We love the look of a long narrow leg in a marvellous slim boot, but we've got our eye on width now" (1968a). The voice may also be authoritatively dismissive: "Anything does not go. Bell bottoms do not go with a pants suit." (1971a). It provides all the news, what is fit to wear and what is not.

As Point of View condenses the information previously given in features on beauty, accessories, and clothing, it prepares the reader (sets the mood) for the fashions that are to come. Point of View is written in a kind of fashion-writing shorthand, "initiating" (Barthes 1990, 14) the reader with the information needed to translate the fashions shown. Words and phrases from Point of View are also used repetitively as titles and slogans in the fashion spreads.

Throughout this article I will be referring to Point of View as though it were authored, pen to paper, by the editor-in-chief. This is usually not the case, as the creation of a magazine is a collaborative effort, involving editorial, art, and advertising departments, among others. However, what is finally produced is fashion—as defined by the editor-in-chief. The voice of Point of View is the voice of *Vogue*, resonant with the particular inflections of the editor-in-chief. Thus I will acknowledge Vreeland, Mirabella, and Wintour as its successive "authors."

Tie violet ribbon in your hair.

[Diana Vreeland], *Vogue*, September 1, 1968

The attitude is attractive, casual, nonchalant—the attitude of jeans and sweaters.

[Grace Mirabella], *Vogue*, September 1973

> Leather still emerges with a tough, give-'em-hell attitude, which should satisfy the Thelma and Louise in every woman....
>
> [Anna Wintour], *Vogue*, September 1991

The Editors

In distinguishing between writers and editors, between style as "absolutely singular speech" and writing as "collective speech," Barthes asserts that:

> the editor invests nothing of himself in his speech, nothing of his deep psychology; he simply conforms to a certain conventional and regulated tone...by which, moreover, we immediately recognize a fashion magazine (Barthes 1990, 227–228).

While acknowledging that the language of fashion is largely formalized with its own conventions, I have found that Vreeland, Mirabella, and Wintour developed distinctly individual *styles*. It is, for example, impossible to confuse a late 1970s Point of View by Mirabella with any one produced by Vreeland. Each bears the signature of the editor, even as the look of the magazine reflects her vision. The written editorial styles that Vreeland, Mirabella, and Wintour have crafted with the common tools provided by the existing verbal "fashion system," are examined in the following pages.

Diana Vreeland, Editor-in-Chief 1963–1970

In life, and as an editor, Diana Vreeland was heroic and adventurous. Fashion was the tool with which she realized fantasies and made fictions real. She celebrated the incredible transformative aspect of clothing and encouraged others to do so. The following proclamation is a characteristic one:

> To transform yourself into a Romany princess is divine—if it turns you up and puts you at your ease. But don't get lost in someone else's dream: there is enough adventure in fashion to find your own (1970a).

Vreeland's penchant was for dream clothes—costume, as opposed to "real" clothing. Her preference was for the unique creations of the haute couture. It should not be surprising that ready-to-wear, with its "plain-spoken" quality, was not favored by a woman who firmly believed that individuality and idiosyncrasy could, and should, be eloquently expressed through clothing. In the captions of her fashion spreads, it

is typical to find comments such as "we added the tassels" or "shown without matching belt." Such adjustments are not only Vreeland-isms but are also in keeping with the free spirit of the 1960s. Similar comments are not found in Mirabella's 1970s *Vogue*s that plug for "all of a tone" and "total look" dressing (1972) and suggest that the reader "let the designer do the putting together" (1977). Just as Vreeland and Mirabella defined the needs of women differently, so they viewed fashion and its functions variously. Vreeland stressed inventiveness; Mirabella emphasized selectivity and smart shopping.

It must be acknowledged that while Vreeland did encourage individual expression in her texts, her own voice and predilections, indeed her signature, are vividly affixed to Point of View. Mirabella figured herself as a "democratic" editor, concerned with fashion "for all," in contrast with Vreeland. In Vreeland's *Vogue*, democratic values relate not to the masses (mainly serviced by the ready-to-wear industry) but to the freedom of expression, however fantastic, associated with the couture. Point of View, before and during Vreeland's editorship, ran under the title "Vogue's Eye View." The Table of Contents each September noted that the collection report was by Diana Vreeland, and each of Vreeland's September Point of Views is signed with her curvaceous and bold initials: DV. "Eye View" is a fitting title, as the opinions and the language in which they are expressed are so very much the personal voice of an "I." The subjects of movement, the exotic, the historic, and the literary appear throughout Eye View, the fashion spreads, and in Vreeland's memoirs.

"High" culture, particularly literature and the fine arts, informs much of Vreeland's *Vogue*. Allusions to Chaucer, Proust, and Rimbaud spice her distinctive texts with an inspirational and exuberant pitch. Vreeland's texts are always moving toward crescendo. Barthes recognizes "culture's" place in fashion's rhetoric as "simply represent[ing] a reasonable degree of social advancement" (Barthes 1990, 241). This suggests that culture is a convention of fashion writing tied to the editor's perception of the reader's acculturation rather than to a personal style. I read the "culture" in Vreeland's texts as distinctive.

The text of Vreeland's *Vogue* is the least "poor" (Barthes 1990, 236) of the three editors'. Its "cultural" richness is especially evident when compared with Mirabella's texts which have virtually no allusions to high or low culture, and with Wintour's which are rife with references to popular culture. Vreeland's *Vogue* is the most poetic in style, and it combines, with gusto, many of the characteristics of fashion writing identified by Barthes, including use of metaphor, alliteration, and "mythic" language.

Vreeland sees colors with names like "café-au-lait" and "dubonnet." She discovers that long coats transform the wearer into a "1970s clothed nude descending a staircase, swinging through the streets,

swinging all over the world" (1970b). An invocation to "tie violet ribbon in your hair" (1968a) has the syncopation of poetic verse. Vreeland's texts are like nuggets of ore to be mined for suggestions that have the potential of transforming life, through fashion, into a glittering and marvelous adventure.

Grace Mirabella, Editor-in-Chief 1973–1987[6]

Whereas Vreeland was concerned with potentiality, Mirabella focused on function and practicality. Vreeland wrote: "In the evening, we go east of the sun and west of the moon—we enter the world of fantasy" (1970a). Mirabella asserts: "When you come to evening this year, you do not come to another planet" (1971a). Mirabella fashioned herself as a champion of "real" clothes for real (American) women. Her down-to-earth concerns focused not only on the wearing but on the acquiring of fashion. Mirabella's Point of View is designed to be a consumer's guide for "shopping, buying, and wearing" (1981).

As a guide, Mirabella's Point of View participates in the didactic function of fashion language, as identified by Barthes (Barthes 1990, 6). A statement such as: "End of lecture. Beginning of new season—next page" (1973) suggests that Mirabella was conscious of her didacticism. Besides being characteristic of Mirabella's style, this dogmatic stance was perhaps a necessary editorial position in a decade—the "anti-fashion" 1970s—during which "the multiplication of styles created an impression of total anarchy" (Boucher 1987, 434).

Mirabella's editorials countered fashion anarchy with practical fashion guidance for recessionary times. Her premise was that the value of clothes related to their functionalism. Thus, it was important to shop smartly and get what you paid for—clothes that adapted to the many facets of a modern, active woman's lifestyle. She concluded that the role of *Vogue* was to provide information with which readers could make good consumer decisions. After all:

> If you don't know a hen from a fryer, you're going to wind up with a sauteed cardboard. And if you don't know a narrow line from a right one, you're going to find yourself with a turkey on your hands (1975).

No peacocks for Mirabella.

Point of View, under Mirabella, was written in the (quasi) style of a business brief, focusing on "dollar-for-dollar" value and "real-life" practicality. The tone is part feminist, part consumer advocate, and part "auntie"[7] figure; witness: "catch yourself in a rear-view mirror before you walk out of the store" (1981).

Mirabella stated that she wanted her *Vogue* to be "information-packed" (Mirabella 1995, 154), and she succeeded—her Point of View is more dense than either Vreeland's or Wintour's. It is not dense with things fictive, historic, or poetic, however. Rather she referred to "green stamps" (1974) and styles that were "our pick for Ford of the year" (1977). Clothes are not divine; they are "luxe-y" and easy, they project confidence and bravado. This is the American sportswear look, straightforward, and with the "chic informality" (Mirabella 1995, 154) Mirabella so valued.

Anna Wintour, Editor-in-Chief 1980–Present

In place of the French couture fashions that Vreeland loved and the American ready-to-wear looks that Mirabella favored, the (British) Wintour combines American and European styles into a kind of "international" or "global" fashion. Her first cover (November 1988) featured a model in jeans and a beaded Lacroix jacket. Wintour has adopted the role of "mix-master" which well suits the retro and street-influenced styles of recent times.

Wintour plays the role of fashion-editor-as-celebrity well, publicly making light of it, but initiating in 1992, the "Letter from the Editor" through which her voice is heard. Her signature is affixed to the "Letter" where, typically, the artists and writers whose work has been commissioned for the issue are highlighted. Art and literature were the lenses through which Vreeland saw and interpreted fashion; Wintour focuses instead on the relation of the world of fashion to the world of art—especially highlighting the trends of the former and the "downtown" scenes of the latter.

Youth and trendiness are featured in Wintour's *Vogue*. Characteristic is kinetic advice such as: "One bold stroke of ruby red lipstick creates forties glamor. In a few seconds a temporary tattoo provides downtown attitude" (1992). Wintour has stated that her approach is "to have enough reality in the magazine not to lose a lot of readers, or a lot of people who aren't as hip as everybody else or as willing to accept change" (Sischy 1993, 101). *Vogue*'s attention to "hipness" under Wintour is in keeping with the quest, on the part of the media, to define and woo the so-called x-generation of twenty-something consumers.

Under Wintour, Point of View has been used as a space in which to explore and define trends with essays entitled "The Cutting Edge" (January 1992) and "What's Modern Now?" (January 1993) by Suzy Menkes. Though Point of View has traditionally been the vehicle of the editor, Wintour's role is not diminished by her use of Menkes. Rather, Menkes joins *Vogue*'s stable of contributing artists and writers—while Wintour's voice is sounded in the Letter from the Editor.

Like Menkes, Wintour is, by her own definition, a journalist (Sischy 1993, 101). Her journalistic style differs from Vreeland's poetry and

the spare, business style of the Heloise-like Mirabella. Wintour's Point of View is sprinkled with references to icons of popular culture like Madonna, Twiggy, and Marlene Dietrich. She cites (big fashion) names such as Lacroix and Christy Turlington, as well as quotes, in journalistic fashion, designers and industry professionals. Wintour meticulously traces trends such as: "Ralph Lauren's Russian romanticism; Jean-Paul Gaultier's textured tribute to Hasidism and Rifat Ozbek's multi-cultural mélange" (1993). The trends Wintour identifies are the currency of a modern, fast-paced, and increasingly international world.

...Words strain,
Crack and sometimes break, under the burden,
Under the tension, slip, slide, perish,
Decay with imprecision, will not stay in place,
Will not stay still.
T.S. Eliot, "Burnt Norton," from *The Four Quartets*

The Language of Fashion

Fashion language (or "Vogue speak") is a fascinating subject. It is colorful, inventive, and over-blown: "Furs are to die"; colors are "tauped up"; looks are "leotard simple." Barthes speaks of the rhetoric of fashion as "a very broad formulary" (Barthes 1990, 186). The consistency and tenacity of this "formulary" is confirmed by the relevance of Barthes' 1958–1959 study of French magazines to my own of American *Vogue* from 1968–1993.

Fashion rhetoric, like the larger world of fashion which Gilles Lipovetsky describes as a "cocktail of images, sounds, and meanings," (Lipovetsky 1994, 160) is concocted of smaller parts such as metaphor and alliteration. I have organized these smaller parts into four categories: visual, oral, emphatic, and popular, in order to identify some of them better. They serve to fulfill the two major functions of fashion language identified by Barthes: to "denote," or describe an actual garment, or to "connote," or relate the object to the world.[8] Neither the functions of language nor the categories I have defined are absolute. A single word can fulfill different functions; thus an alliterative description can fulfill both oral and emphatic functions.

Adjectives and metaphors are often used to convey the visual aspects of fashion—"image-clothing." The color, dimension, and style of a garment (its parts or the whole) are thus made vivid. In addition to the characteristically colorful adjectives which typify Vogue-speak ("seraglio shimmer"), there exists a whole other subcategory of "adjectival substances" created by hyphenation. Thus there exists the "knit-two-purl-two look" (1970b) and the "have-it-your-way philosophy" (1993).

Metaphor aids in the visualization of style by linking a look or a garment to a point of reference outside of the world of fashion as in "red stockings à la the Wife of Bath" (1969b). While metaphors and adjectives help the reader to "see" fashion, the use of alliteration sounds the voice of fashion as it describes the current mode: "Drifty. Dreamy. Wow plus sigh."[9] Mental tongues are tied around the "written-garment" in the September 1, 1968, issue of *Vogue* where "fringe is flicking, flashing, flying" whereas the "sixties pop of patent" adds rhythm to Wintour's prose in 1990. In 1977 rhyme highlights the arrival of "wonderful new flings-of-things." Alliteration and rhyme help to syncopate the text and to lend it an oral texture.

The third major function of the language of fashion is the emphatic one. Fashion's rhetoric is one of absolutes and extremes, allowing only for bangs, never for a whimper. Emphasis is achieved mainly through hyperbole and repetition. This description of coats that are "bigger, furrier, luxe-ier than anyone's, anywhere, ever"[10] is typical of the hyperbolic statements common to Point of View. There are several subcategories of repetition. Repetition can be alliterative or fixed mantra-like on a single word: "belt it tight, tight, tight at the waist" (1969a). An aberration of repetition is multiplication: "Furs are flat, fuzzy, fluffy, puffy, silky, short, long, patterned, coloured" (1968a). The yoking together of seemingly unrelated topics ("new and recherché" [1969b]), after the fashion of multiplication, is known as parataxis. Barthes uses the example: "She likes studying and surprise parties, Pascal, Mozart and cool jazz" (Barthes 1990, 225)—quite a heady "cocktail."

Barthes' jazz is countered by Wintour's: "shiny leather motorcycle-style clothes with a rock 'n' roll/Brando glamour" (1991). Popular language and references to popular culture are often used in Point of View. I use the term "popular language" rather than Barthes' "poor rhetoric" (Barthes 1990, 236–7) or Ellen McCraken's "mythic language" (McCraken 1993, 77) because popular implies mass or multiplicity. I place the everyday maxims, proverbs, and euphemisms that appear in Point of View under the heading of popular language.

Barthes makes an important separation of the authoritative fashion editor from the "mass of…users (which would be the equivalent of the 'speaking mass' which produces language)" (Barthes 1990, 215) in the *production* of fashion language and writing. Expressions such as "any woman worth her salt" (1970b) and "poufs, crinolines, and all that jazz" (1988) have their roots in a popular parlance used by readers and consciously invoked by editors to broaden the appeal of their messages.

In the photographic spreads, where images create the main narrative, wordplay hones the message, drawing attention to details. For example, the titles accompanying a spread on coats in the September 1968 issue of *Vogue* read: "Coats/all wrapped up," and "Coats/on top of it all."[11] This type of wordplay has been called childlike. Barthes characterizes

this language as a borrowing from "...a vulgarized literary tradition, either from rhyming games...or from commonplace comparisons" (Barthes 1990, 237). I find this use of language interesting precisely in the way it self-consciously combines the "high" with the popular. Moreover this type of yoking in some ways mirrors the relationship between the idealized, distant image and its popular, verbal denominator (coat, glove) which makes it understandable and accessible.

Editorial self-consciousness is one of the most subtle and interesting features of Point of View. The language of fashion, like the clothing it describes, is ever changing. Thus the editor must constantly redefine the words that she uses to write fashion. Changes in fashion language are marked in Mirabella's *Vogue* with the greatest frequency. For example, the reader is warned against accepting "old-fashioned" definitions in 1976. There is also a pause in the September 1977 Point of View to note that "soft...is one of those tricky umbrella words that can mean anything and everything" and an ensuing redefinition of the word.

Fashion language can be season specific. "Edgy" is the term of choice for the recent Spring 1996 collections. In September 1970 Vreeland wrote that "Variety is the great big glorious word in fashion right now." In 1991 Wintour noted that: "eclectic is the buzzword." Words can be as changeable as hemlines. In 1969 readers were informed of "the eclipse of 'groovy' which now sounds very Lawrence Welk."[12] Names of trends often come from popular language, or enter into it, as "grunge" did. In her essay on fashion images, Kathy Myers focuses on the instability created by the media's ability to produce new meanings (Myers 1987, 58). The same is true of fashion language, which needs constantly to be redefined in relation to new clothes and changing environments.

The so-called "verbiage of fashion" (Caen 1989, 29) is countered, to a great degree, by the conventions of fashion language that have been identified above. In their survey of English women, Ballaster et al., discovered that the *language* of fashion was a source of pleasure to readers. They reported that "...when talking about magazines, women endlessly and diligently parody and mimic them, displaying their own literacy in and mastery of its generic conventions" (Ballaster, et al., 35).

The language of fashion, a popular one, is owned and can be enjoyed by all, while its images are often rarified, and garments often unobtainable.

The Tone

Vreeland's exaltative and lyrical exclamations, Mirabella's practical narrative guidance, and Wintour's snappy, savvy journalistic style are distinctive forms of the oral culture perpetuated through women's magazines. This culture can rightly be designated oral, although it is

written because of the "write-speak" (Ferguson 1983, 165) style which is its distinguishing feature. Ballaster et al., note that "...many analysts have been struck by the intimate tone employed to address the reader, the cozy invocation of a known commonality between 'we women'" (Ballaster et al., 9). This "chatty" tone is related to the style of writing known as "personalizing" (Ferguson 1983, 165). Fashion writing is specifically written for women in a tone that is complicit, based on a shared interest in fashion.

Most of the current scholarship on women's magazines focuses on their "feminocentric" (Ballaster et al., 169) bias and on the images of women in them.[13] The tone of women's magazines has also been the subject of much study. Barthes defines this tone as "maternal" (Barthes 1990, 241) (which is perhaps an accurate characterization for the dictatorial late 1950s), but today "the idea of the magazine as friend" (Ballaster et al., 1991, 125) is ascendant. This tendency can be dated to the late 1960s when "magazines became less dogmatic and more interactive" (Craik 1994, 52). The editorial voice of *Vogue* in the period from 1968 to 1993 is positive, friendly without being too warm, and, importantly, it is an informed voice. The editor is privy to "insider-information" which justifies her authority to tell the reader what "everybody" is wearing, report what "we" (the editors of the magazine) like, and suggest what "you" (the reader) should buy.

Feminists have criticized the advertising and editorial portrayal of women in fashion magazines as being misinformed and/or misogynous. Unlike newspapers, which are characterized by "empirical and analytic reporting," magazines use "ideal and emotive novelisation" as their means of appeal (Ballaster et al., 1991, 48). Novelization shifts the focus from what is (facts) to what could or should be (conjecture). Fashion magazines necessarily offer a fractured world view because their focus is one subject. (The use of parataxis in fashion writing emphasizes this fragmentation.) Fashion magazines present not a whole world-view but an utopian one.

Though images of women in fashion magazines are sometimes fractured too, the fashion magazine, as an institution, is seen to unify. Naomi Wolf believes that women's magazines represent "women's mass culture" and asserts that they "cater to that delicious sense of impersonal female solidarity...bring[ing] out of the closet women's lust for chat across the barriers of potential jealousy and prejudgement" (Wolf 1991, 70). Similarly, Diana Fuss notes that: "the entire fashion industry operates as one of the few institutionalized spaces where women can look at women with cultural impunity" (Fuss 1992, 713). Some, though, would argue that the institutionalized language of fashion provides women with stereotypical ways of talking about each other as well.

Fashion magazine editors, like editors of technical journals, use jargon that is specific to their subject. Jargon of any kind is thus

"institutionalized." *Vogue* is a primer of fashion language, but what I have found is that Vreeland, Mirabella, and Wintour have each created separate voices that can also be learned. Thus it is possible to mimic fashion language not only in a general manner, but quite specifically—Vreeland's "divine," Mirabella's "ease." The way in which the editor has "dressed" up fashion's rhetoric has changed the way we talk about it.

Notes

1. This book was written collectively.
2. A recent trend at Condé Nast is the reproduction of archival images in magazines such as *Vogue* and *Allure*. This attests to the power of retro on current fashions and also, more generally, to the power of the image.
3. See Ellen McCraken for distinctions among magazine genres, such as weeklies, glossies, and service magazines.
4. See Craik 1994, 55.
5. References to September Point of Views between 1968 and 1993 will be credited parenthetically in the text. Between 1968 and 1972 *Vogue* was published twice in September, on the first and the fifteenth. September 1 issues are designated (19a) and September 15 issues are designated (19b). Although Point of View has appeared variously in *Vogue* as: Vogue's Eye View, Vogue's Point of View, Vogue/Point of View, it will be referred to as Point of View throughout.
6. Mirabella was promoted to Editor in 1971 and became Editor-in-Chief in 1973.
7. See Ballaster et al.1991, 118. The "auntie" is more generally referred to as the "agony aunt." She dispenses advice in regard to readers' queries.
8. Barthes' fashion system is divided into A and B ensembles. A ensembles are denotative; B ensembles are connotative. See 3.12, 40.
9. n.a., *Vogue*, March 15, 1968, 130.
10. n.a., "Paris Report," *Vogue* September 15, 1971, 62.
11. n.a., *Vogue*, September 1968, 632, 628.
12. n.a., *Vogue*, April 15, 1969, 82.
13. See Craik, 50.

References

Ballaster, Ros, Margaret Beetham, Elizabeth Frazer, and Sandra Hebron, eds. 1991. *Women's Worlds: Ideology, Femininity and the Woman's Magazine*. London: Macmillan.

Barthes, Roland. 1990. *The Fashion System*, translated by Matthew Ward and Richard Howard. Berkeley: University of California Press.

Boucher, Francois. 1987. *20,000 Years of Fashion*. New York: Harry N. Abrams.

Caen, Jeanette J. 1989. *Facets of Fashion in The New York Times*. New York: The New York Times Company.

Craik, Jennifer. 1994. *The Face of Fashion*. New York: Routledge.

Eliot. T.S. 1958. *The Complete Poems and Plays*. New York: Harcourt, Brace and Company.

Ferguson, Marjorie. 1983. *Forever Feminine: Women's Magazines and the Cult of Femininity*. London: Heinemann.

Fuss, Diana. 1992. "Fashion and the Homospectorial Look." *Critical Inquiry* 18, pp. 713–37.

Harris, Daniel. 1993. "Some Reflections on the Facial Expressions of Fashion Models: 100 Years of *Vogue*." *Salmagundi* Spring, pp. 128–40.

Lipovetsky, Gilles. 1994. *The Empire of Fashion*, foreword by Richard Sennett. Princeton: Princeton University Press.

McCraken Ellen. 1993. *Decoding Women's Magazines: From Mademoiselle to Ms*. New York: St. Martin's Press.

Mirabella, Grace with Judith Warner. 1995. *In and Out of Vogue*. New York: Doubleday.

Myers, Kathy. 1987. "Fashion 'n' Passion." In *Looking On*, edited by Rosemary Betterton. New York: Pandora.

Sischy, Ingrid. 1993. "Anna Wintour: Front Row and Centered." *Interview* December 1993, pp. 98–101, 135.

Vreeland, Diana. 1984. *D.V.* , edited by George Plimpton and Christopher Hemphill. New York: Alfred A. Knopf.

Wolf, Naomi. 1991. *The Beauty Myth*. New York: William Morrow.

Fashion Theory, Volume 1, Issue 3, pp.261–278
Reprints available directly from the Publishers.

Texture and Taboo: The Tyranny of Texture and Ease in the J. Crew Catalog

Matthew DeBord

Matthew DeBord writes frequently about books, art, culture, fashion, and style. His work has appeared in *frieze*, *Publishers Weekly*, and *Nka: Journal of Contemporary African Art* (where he is an editor). He has also published three New York City guidebooks: *The Irreverent Guide to Manhattan*, *Manhattan by Night* (both from Frommer's), and the *Spin Underground USA Guide to New York*. He is currently working on a series of essays about reviewing.

After starting out as a sort of poor man's Brooks Brothers and a rich man's Lands' End marketing simple, traditional styles of clothing to a standard-issue direct-mail crowd—those living far from style-fraught urban centers—J. Crew has in the last five years transformed its catalog from a document that depicted smiling WASPS in conventionally convivial, invigorating settings (on the lawn, at the beach, lugging logs through the snow while a frisky golden retriever lopes along in tow) to an instrument for promulgating a design vision that has become almost hermetically singular. The catalog is instantly identifiable, breathtakingly unlike *Vogue* or *Harper's Bazaar*, distant from the capricious districts of high fashion, but equally unlike the dowdy publications circulated

links levity

Reading of tycoon trend to the backyard putting green, fairway-and-green. . . even entire nine-hole course. . . our friend, not outfaced, uses the resources at hand.

by other direct-mail catalog merchandizers. A J. Crew *mise-en-scène* could be nothing else—athletic, limber, youthful, and above all else relaxed. The game, for those who study the catalog, has become one of distinguishing the clothes from the art direction; this, however, is a little like falling prey to a bad case of Cartesian dualism, trying to separate the mind (catalog design and shoot styling) from the body (the product—clothes).

It's an impossible, and in fact deeply flawed, undertaking, so thoroughly is the ostensible merchandise implicated in its catalog presentation. J. Crew's clothing is meaningless—worse, *disappointing*—without its distinctive context; in the world that dwells between the catalog's covers, an inviolable epistemology of densely enmeshed, interrelated elements is seamlessly established. It will not deconstruct. It is, for all intents and purposes, perfect, and perfectly alluring. Men comment that a fashion-mag goddess like Stella Tennent does nothing for them ("Too unreal, too unattainable") but that a nameless J. Crew minx, daubed with nothing more than sunscreen, lights their fires. Predatory eyeballs everywhere popped with the debut, on page 76 of the Spring Preview 1997 catalog, of not one but *two* nipples, glimpsed gauzily through a delicate camisole, and unairbrushed chest freckles, all artfully delivered in a knuckle-gnawing black-and-white spread that featured J. Crew Intimates, the company's line of women's undergarments. This plausible, posited reality, which of course exists nowhere, bespeaks an almost triumphant confidence, a haughty chutzpah that feels free to take chances that would not only be noticeable in a fashion magazine, but noticeably alienating. Placing a $100 khaki dress on a placidly smirking model (a real-world placid smirk, by the way—affected expressions are outlawed in Crewland) who just happens to be standing next to a wildly expensive ensemble of furniture compliments of Knoll or Herman Miller is, to say the least, a gutsy move. But the "serious" design barely registers, so carefully melded is it with the preeminence of what the models are wearing. Obviously, this is hard labor. Anyone with a design sense, even a severely limited one—could guess that J. Crew keeps its location scouts busy finding "tableaux" against which to layer the company's clothing, as well as finding an assortment of precisely selected objects to lend a humanizing cast to the oftentimes austere compositions.

The clothes themselves are, by design, unremarkable. There are periodic percolations of stylistic adventurism. Who could forget Autumn 1995's velvet episode, an evident homage to Donna Karan, or the recent back-of-the-catalog references to Tom Ford, Miu Miu, and Patrick Demarchelier, particularly the sudden appetite for monochromatic layerings: orange on orange, pale blue on pale blue? A little Dolce & Gabbana has even crept into the layouts for the usually phlegmatic menswear sections—skinny white boys, shaggy hair, too-tight argyle sweater vests, and chunky black Buddy Holly specs. But no one is going

Figure 1
© J. Crew

Facing the ske
protagonist mani
in shetland ja

to confuse J. Crew with Anna Sui. Still, a component of the J. Crew product mix, both practically *and* in presentation, has become associated with a brand of New York/Los Angeles casual cool. One can wear a pair of simple, wool J. Crew trousers and feel either formal or fanciful. This is the message delivered by the catalog's layouts, which shift from austere, predominantly white backgrounds through which the clothes drift, colorful puffs of consumer potential, to elegant depictions of relaxed models in airy lofts determined to evoke decided responses of comfort and ease. To prevent all of this from becoming too monotonous, J. Crew's design group has lately taken to what might be termed the "Underwear Angle." It began a few years back with a moderately disrobed guy chattering on the phone amid his shed threads, unselfconsciously outfitted in boxer shorts, socks, a shirt, and an unknotted tie. Expanding on this "End of the Workday" theme, Crew has developed a whole weekend aesthetic that involves a mixture of loungewear, underwear, footwear, and outerwear, with models shown camped out on stoops and shuffling through the supermarket wearing hodgepodged ensembles that almost no one in their right mind would venture out of the house in. However, ease—the willful denial of any measure of self-consciousness, a distilled confidence that dressing decisions made to meet the day, no matter how wacky, are correct—is the mainstay of the J. Crew aesthetic. The assumption is that a consumer will accept the fantasy of confidence articulated by the catalog and not shrink from buying the flannel pajamas, the polar fleece pullover, the rollneck sweater, the red union suit and the demolition boots, and will further not shrink from assembling them all into a god-awful *mélange* suitable for sitting on the stoop on a crisp fall Sunday to sift through *The New York Times*.

Emphasis on Ease

In the pleasantly rumpled framework of the Underwear Angle or the more overtly butch presentation of, say, a late-spring road trip featuring the J. Crew Boys in their flannel-lined blue jeans, boxy plaid shirts, and distressed leather jackets (on a route miles from a major highway, where one can still get those dinky bottles of Coke from a glass-windowed machine in front of an Esso gas station) this emphasis on ease posits a "Gestalt of the Casual," where neurosis (read: fashion) is subsumed by nostalgia. The J. Crew model—a stand-in for the J. Crew *Weltanschauung*—looks blissfully, unreflectively at ease in his or her underwear, looks at ease in the muddy outdoors, looks at ease leaping from a catamaran, looks at ease reading some moldy old book, looks at ease in the settings that pass for professional life, looks at ease dabbing fries in a puddle of ketchup. Significantly, this visual rhetoric of ease emphasizes not only the intrinsic relaxation that will flow from the clothes, if they are purchased, but also the *transportability* of this ease.

Figure 2

A source of tremendous anxiety for American consumers, and especially for American professionals who are compelled to adopt a prescribed wardrobe of respectability for office life, is the prospect of having to change clothes for different social functions. If J. Crew can offer a trouser-and-sweater combination that can carry a working woman from office to dinner to the theater, or to whatever else the world might throw her way, then the company will doubtless be able to convince that woman that she will be well-served by J. Crew's policy of portable ease. Crew ups the ante, however, devising mild variations on its eminently portable designs, so that the prospect of changing, say, for dinner, becomes less daunting. It's no longer a question of switching from a Calvin Klein pantsuit to a Mizrahi gown; a girl can just cast off the trousers and slip into a skirt, lose the flats, and add a pair of heels. The notion of a day regulated by fashion, and by varying subsets of fashion, is replaced by the more subtle tyranny of gentle, textural decisions. In this manner, ease is transported from day to evening simply by replacing gray wool with satin or by exchanging a white-collared blouse for a cropped turtleneck. In the catalog's imagery, the ease of decision necessary to achieve the very portability of ease *itself* is reinforced by the absence of showy pose, the lack of structured postures. Everything despite the elaborate logic of its construction, despite the layers of hard work that have led to its presentation—is made to look effortless.

Vanquished to the neurotic, jittery, ill-at-ease realm of the fashion magazine are those depictions of people wearing too much makeup, too many layers, exhibiting too much shine or crimp, too many visible fetishes. The J. Crew catalog represents the most reactionary response imaginable to the stylistic anxiety provoked by fashion rags, an antidote to an overdesigned frenzy for people who want to believe that their taste is linked with an untrammeled self-confidence, that the two are mutually supportive categories uncontaminated by fashionable temptations. "Style" and "fashion," in the J. Crew worldview, are thereby disconnected, effectively liberating the catalog from competition with the fashion magazines.

The fashion magazines persist in their desire to describe, promote, and prescribe. The J. Crew catalog is much more singular, supplying an experience of viewership more akin to music videos, but with the establishment of a visual continuity that designates its own self-perpetuating structure. Editorial really doesn't exist (though the company maintains a department dedicated to it), apart from the obscure occasional snippets of text: "Links levity . . . Reading of tycoon trend to the backyard putting green...even entire nine-hole course, our friend, not outfaced, uses the resources at hand"[1] paired with a photo of a slackerish-looking punk, in flannel robe, pajama bottoms, and ski hat, putting on a square of Astroturf in front of his brownstone, while a kid in orange polar fleece and a ski cap, holds the flagstick; there is no cup for the ball to fall into. Art direction *omnia est*. This explains why people will pour over the catalog, flipping through it again and again, enthusi-

astically awaiting the next installment (and they are frequent, with new catalogs mailed out as often as twice as month), long after the latest issue of *Elle* has been tossed, unread, into the magazine rack. Via the catalog, identity becomes texture. *Mise-en-scène* becomes texture. Clothing—photographed, arranged, styled, worn, and shed—becomes texture, in a format normally antithetical to tactility. Everything in the J. Crew catalog is homogeneously blended into the publication's ideology of texture and ease. Nothing exists in relief.

It's this abnegation of conventional fashion motives—and the canon of fashion representation (show the *clothes*)—that comforts the "average" J. Crew customer and ensures that he or she will keep coming back. Clothes that are so unremarkable in their composition—their *actual*, as opposed to attributed, composition—will inevitably fail to deliver on the design promise associated with their deceptively over-determined presentation. The customer, therefore, will continue to maintain a fascination with THE CATALOG and will return, relentlessly, for more, in the vain hope that the the J. Crew vision will materialize once the shirts have arrived.

A Little Background Music

J. Crew has been in business since the early 1980s. It started out as a clearing house for *echt* preppy styles at a time when that look was experiencing its runaway popularization via *The Preppy Handbook* and the emergence of Ralph Lauren's Polo line as a mass-market cultural phenomenon. (Ralph plowed the road for The Gap and Banana Republic, along with a host of downmarket imitators.) J. Crew quickly recognized that it had a chance to influence a market that it had previously been able only to interpret. "Preppy" style, or the American "Ivy League" look, had been in hiatus since the late 1950s and early 1960s, when its association with the Kennedys and (as Graham Marsh has pointed out in his catalog of Blue Note album-cover art published in 1991 by Chronicle Books) black jazz musicians, who outfitted themselves in Brooks Brothers oxfords and olive poplin suits, was supplanted by an invasion of European fashion.

By the late 1970s, fashion had become, in the minds of many Americans, pretty loony; the scene was ripe for a reactionary, and this role fell naturally to Lauren, whose Polo line out-WASPed the WASP staples it aped. He charged more for a pair of chinos or a polo shirt than any self-respecting, thrifty WASP would ever pay, but in the process opened up a field of overt product identification and obsessive identity maintenance that would eventually prompt a subrebellion. Many people liked the idea of what he was up to—abhored synthetics, adored 100 percent cotton, disliked the extremes of fashion, lionized comfort, and wanted their clothes to outlast the millennium—but hated the stupid little pony he insisted on sticking on seemingly everything he manufactured,

Matthew DeBord

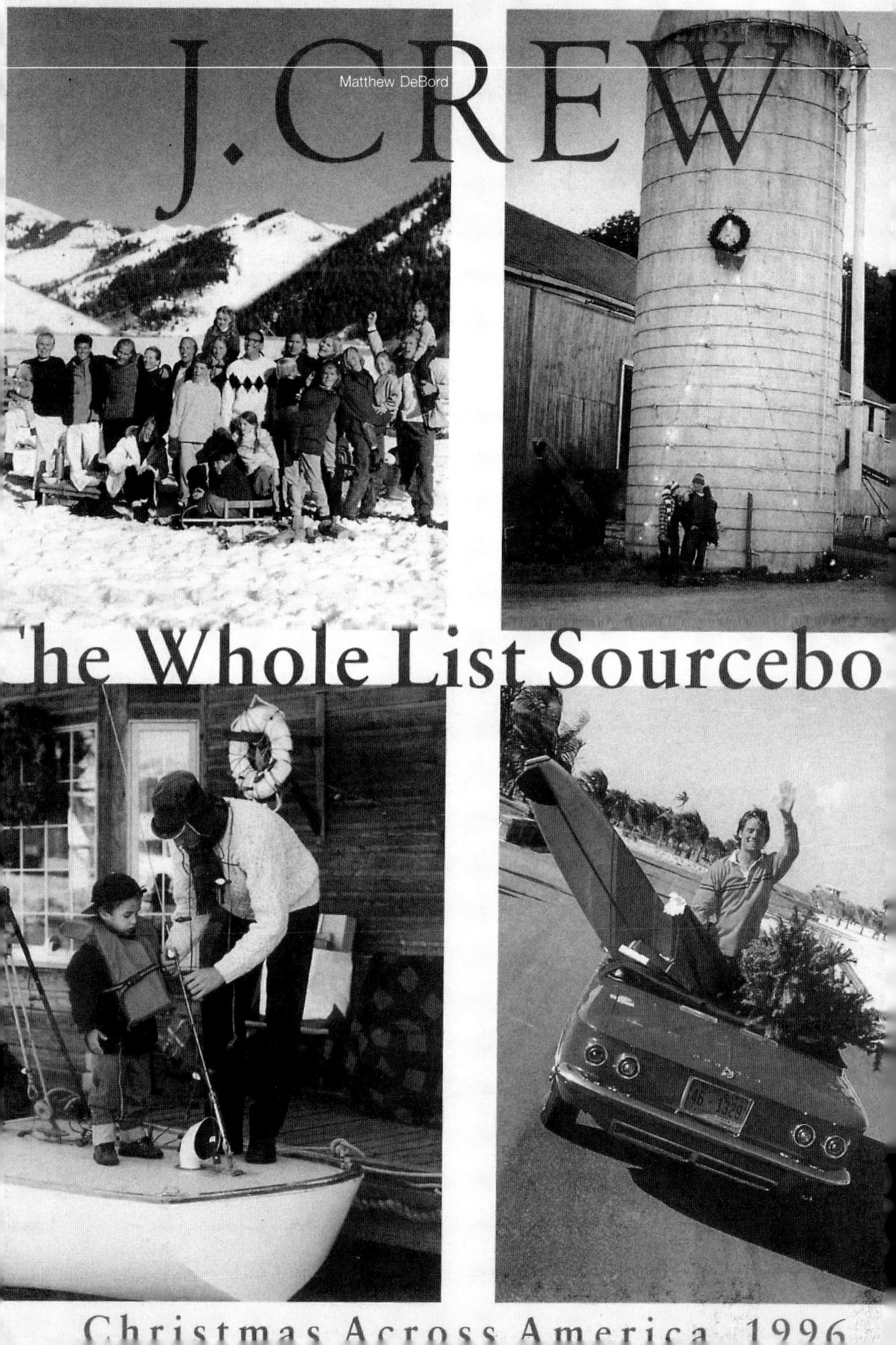

from shirts to socks. Enter J. Crew, with the understanding that there was a whole host of potential customers who shared Lauren's interest in the Ivy look, but who also knew that they were stuck between Lauren's social climbing and L. L. Bean's industrial-strength indifference to anything that resembled style. One could, during the mid-1980s, spend hours digging through the Bean catalog and find *nothing* black, much less a model who looked younger than 40. The style appealed, but the work required to possess it was demoralizing: the exhausting search for Duck Head chinos and the endless digging around in thrift shops for castoff Brooks blazers and suits, which at that time had not begun to show up in significant numbers. Women were in special trouble, since very few retailers were offering simple, functional clothes of the sort that are now commonly available in the post-Prada, neo-Halston marketplace.

The Scene Shifts, the Times Change

The J. Crew catalog, when it first began to appear in the mailboxes of those people who had been mainstays of the Bean catalog, came like a bolt from the blue. Here was the answer. The clothes were cheaper than Polo, they were unadorned, they bespoke confidence and, even then, ease rather than pretense and imitation. And, of course, the catalog was vaguely similar to a fashion magazine but without the offputting threat of heavy-duty art direction. It was all a little too Bruce Weber in those days, but it provided a viable alternative to just about everything else out there. And perhaps best of all for its original enthusiasts, it endorsed an antishopping ethic: the entire exercise of fulfilling those first J. Crew fantasies could be conducted on the phone. No leaving home, no combat with other consumers. It was the advent of virtual style. It was gladly domestic. Nothing interfered with the vital relaxation of the customer.

A whole alternative landscape that plies this consummately post-modern trade is now emerging. One can, without leaving home, surf from J. Crew (the guru and arbiter of it all, and incidentally where the clothes come from) to Crate & Barrel (where the overstuffed but tastefully unadorned chairs and sofa come from) to Smith & Hawken (where the gardening stuff comes from) to Starbucks (where the indispensable coffee comes from) to L. L. Bean (where everything else comes from) to IKEA (where you can buy it all *at once*).

Mail-order used to mean dowdy, as in Sears–Roebuck stylelessness and industrial-strength presentation. It now means *reliably* stylish. It used to mean cheap; it now competes with the pricier designers for customers. It used to mean simple pieces to companion with more "designed" outfits; it now has no reservation about clothing customers from head to toe. And perhaps most significantly, catalog merchandizing used to mean sticking with the catalog. J. Crew, however, has opened

Figure 3

stores, a terrific risk when you think about it—there's no way these places can live up to the world showcased in the catalog. This is arguably why the company's South Street Seaport store in lower Manhattan, while successful among the tourist crowds, never stoked the fires of consumer excitation in the way that the SoHo store has. The South Street store was a material supplement to the catalog but not a substitute. The SoHo store, which opened to much hoopla in November of 1996, *is* the catalog given substance. Unlike clothiers who began with shops and then developed catalog businesses, mining the same stylistic territory as J. Crew—Brooks Brothers, Paul Stuart, J. Press—Crew began with a spectacular fantasy, developed it to a point of consummate formidability, and only then unleashed it on the material world. This is why, after years with the Crew catalog, the new stores seem a curious letdown, while ambling through Paul Stuart's or Brooks Brothers' Madison Avenue stores seems fantastically disconnected from the experience of leafing through their halfheartedly conceived catalogs.

Your Mom and Dad, They Buy You Clothes

Nowhere is the J. Crew catalog ideology more apparent than in the company's restoration of the peaceful family romance. Whether these romancing families are actual or surrogate is of little consequence; disparate agendas are unified under the Crew umbrella, making loose, youthful groupings of LA skate rats appear as supportive as Frank Gehry's or Mariel Hemingway's actual broods. In any case, no one is at all dolled up. The height of formality, especially in the astounding Christmas 1996 catalog (a document so beautifully and convincingly composed that it should be enshrined somewhere under the rubric of "This Is How to Sell Clothes"), is a tie worn with a flannel houndstooth shirt (though interestingly, Crew has abandoned its line of ties in the catalog, selling them exclusively in the stores).[2]

The debut, in 1995, of a line of children's clothing called "Crewcuts" signaled a further marshaling of the J. Crew design forces against the company's antipode, The Gap, which has lines for babies as well as for children. Gap contra Crew is an interesting struggle, since The Gap has been at pains over the past three or four years to steer its Banana Republic stores away from their former safari/colonial theme toward something that can impede the J. Crew juggernaut. The Gap has been, to a degree, successful, but at the expense of transforming Banana Republic into a component of the J. Crew mythology. With J. Crew, one gets The Gap and Banana Republic at the same time; The Gap and Banana Republic, by contrast, are required to inhabit entirely separate design contexts appealing to distinctly different consumer groups. The Gap's design avatars are required to do twice as much creative work to stay apace of their main stylistic competition.

Men, women, and children—though not yet babies—can happily coexist in Crewland, amid cheer and vigorous health and the almost total absence of competitive cultures, such as hip-hop style or haute couture or fetishwear. The colossal act of denial required to make this disheveled Xanadu work is understandable if one looks to similar developments in Laurenland or Kleinville. The individual shopping experience has, in all of these cases, been invalidated, replaced by the passive acceptance of a single design vision which Lauren and Klein have borrowed or stolen from, respectively, the famous WASP/preppy stores—Brooks and J. Press—(and from Halston and Armani), and which Crew has assembled from a careful analysis of fashion trends, then diluted for integration into Crewland via the catalog. Risky, innovative designers, such as Dirk Bikkembergs and Dries van Noten, are studiously avoided. Flat designers in the good graces of the fashion press (if not the market), such as Karan, are embraced. The Gallianos and Versaces and Gaultiers—and especially the likes of Kawakubo and Miyaki—are rejected outright.

This reductive packaging of American casual style, so influential internationally during the Cold War era, isn't so much offensive as undemocratic. Americans are supposed to like their morality, not their style, to be received. J. Crew, however, has succeeded in short-circuiting that preference, evolving a dictatorship of style that dupes consumers through an ethic of presentation. It is so packed with moral assumptions that to deviate from its carefree dictates is to risk the stressful, neuroticizing inclination to shop that Americans have lately been educated to believe is going to wreck their fragile families and put them in early graves. Apart from the requisite black clothes to lure the New Yorkers, funeral garb is absent from Crewland, as is any other sort of style that might be connected with human trauma.

Hale and Healthy

The J. Crew catalog, then, achieves a notable eradication paired with an equally notable innovation: it banishes neurosis and trauma about what to wear, and it establishes a legitimate textual dimension that integrates all of its various elements. "Every detail of every item is thought about and designed," declares J. Crew Vice-Chairman Emily Woods.[3] Of course, the woman directing this really remarkable exercise must be aware of how drastically *understated* her comment is. This pervasiveness of design in the catalog—the main outlet for the company's design ideology, despite the existence of more than 30 stores nationwide—has sponsored the emergence of a tactility lacking in almost all other visual forums, particularly the fashion magazines. Out of arrangement, styling, pose, and *mise-en-scène* comes literal *feeling*.

Freudian psychoanalysis would commend this development as

J. CREW
Spring 1997

evidence of transference that signals the grafting of the analysand's symptoms onto the analyst. Patients who transfer are on their way to a cure, as the story of psychoanalysis goes. Consumers who accept the J. Crew catalog's alluring tactility, however, are not necessarily on the path to fulfillment; though they might buy a lot of stuff, the aim of the catalog is to provoke them to buy even more. This arrested transference, mediated by masterly visuals and clinched by the catalog's narcotic of implied texture, *is* the catalog's main objective, one that it supplements audaciously through the inclusion of recognizable celebrities, such as Lauren Hutton (an early entry) and Patrick Dempsey (impishly assured star of the Christmas 1996 haberdashery spreads: "Facing the skeptical world of affairs, protagonist manifests confidence, poise, in shetland jacket, donegal trousers").[4]

Touch, the most elusive of senses for catalog merchandizers to tap into, is thus meaningfully contrived in the Crew catalog, promoting a sensual ideology of avid consumerism. It's useful to recognize at this point that J. Crew accomplishes this radical restatement of a catalog's possibilities—this visual conjuring of touch—within the boundaries of conventional printing on paper, while Armani and Lauren must maintain vast physical retail presences in their major markets. To feel Armani, one goes to the store and touches the fabric; to feel J. Crew, one sits at home, leafing through the catalog, the phone close by, the toll-free number on almost every page. This activity—mundane as it may sound—is becoming common among even the most devout fashion junkies and style mavens, regardless of the sort of class distinctions that compelled the old bluebloods to snub Brooks Brothers in the 1980s in favor of L. L. Bean. Holly Brubach, Style Editor for the *New York Times Magazine*, sings the praises of the J. Crew catalog, confessing that she orders something every few months. And the fledgling socialite Clarina Notz announces in *Vogue*: "I wear Calvin, Prada, Joseph, Valentino, Richard Tyler, *and* J. Crew . . . But I would never wear the whole thing together. *Ever*!"[5]

The New Frontier

It is clear that J. Crew has reinvented the direct-mail clothing market via its catalog, but the obvious analysis—that Crew offers not a catalog but a magazine that designates a series of lifestyle decisions (à la Martha Stewart's authoritarianly prescriptive *Living*) is invalid. The J. Crew catalog is anything but a magazine. Precisely because its ideology of an easygoing, "unstyled" textural aesthetic stands in dramatic counterpoint to the overburdened referencing that governs fashion magazines, the catalog represents an inscrutable challenge to the doyens of Seventh Avenue and their print accomplices on Madison. Whether this is a desirable state of affairs for American fashion is an open question, but

Figure 4
© J. Crew

the triumph of sportswear over couture and designer would appear to be almost complete, despite the advent of the urban signature boutique. In New York, America's style capital, this development is particularly evident: with the decline of Barney's, and the sense that Bendel's, Bloomingdale's, and Bergdorf Goodman are trapped in distinctive Manhattan style "eras," the unavailability of a trendsetting retail space to rival Los Angeles' Fred Segal is, to put it mildly, depressing. One can understand why New Yorkers—alienated by downmarket clearing houses like Loehmann's and Filene's, confused by the proliferation of tiny Downtown shops specializing in twentysomething-wear, and frustrated by the haute Eurotrash/celebrity-mongering Italian boutiques springing up on Madison Avenue—would choose to settle for versions of style that don't demand from them an endless reinvestment in the shock of the new. The J. Crew catalog offers this seductive, tactile, bastion of solace and ease to a beleaguered style tribe, and the tribe rewards its anointed dresser with the tribute that it most desires: a villa in Soho and a steady stream of plastic cash.

Rumbling beneath this surface is, if not menace, then a form of modulated, carefree nationalism that seeks, at times dramatically, to distance itself from the taint of foreign style, with the ultimate objective being the trumping of foreign style in spite of foreign style's current ubiquity. To be sure, J. Crew borrows, but its borrowings appear more benign than what, say, Prada is up to with its pillaging of the fashion iconography of the American 1970s. Prada, though essentially concerned with costly basics, is a fashion house, and because it is trapped in that spectacular structure, must reinvent itself incessantly, at times very glibly. This is a survival process that can make the Milanese font of the sleek, the black, and the unadorned in its occasional missteps look a little more like Diesel than it would probably like. J. Crew, however, understands that Eurostyle is basically American casual with a few loony digressions and further understands that it has nothing to worry about. Europeans will, by and large, dress like Americans, in droves, even if Americans become periodically obsessed with European adaptations of American styles. One could argue, for example, that stylistically adventurous Americans are the only people who are going to take Gaultier jeans, with their ridiculous encrustations of goofball references, seriously; the French are going to stick with Levi's. And, ultimately, so are the Americans. Bored to death, however, with classics such as Levi's, Americans will nevertheless enable J. Crew to establish very successful lines of denim. Something obvious, like lining a pair of baggy jeans with polar fleece, is enough to do the trick.

For J. Crew, then, style is a clear means of expressing the national priority, which at base must connect with the mechanisms that spread that priority. For most, American style is linked with freedom, and the J. Crew catalog—without resorting to the usual Laurenisms or Hilfigerisms of plastering the Stars and Stripes on everything in sight

or of bedecking everyone in red, white, and blue—sustains the idea of freedom, in the weave of its catalog aesthetic, at such a lovely, low hum that the political aspect of its message becomes like oxygen, indispensable. This is a very powerful type of trans-McLuhanism—paralleling the catalog's psychological transneuroticism—that acknowledges the medium as the message but then bends the medium back to the meaning the message formerly sought to transmit. There is not one shred of irony to be found anywhere in the J. Crew catalog, even in a recent installment, which showcases a man in clown shoes. In a culture obsessed with the internal coherence not of the artifact—the work of art, the work of literature, the film, or the musical recording, the performance—but of the commentary that the artifact prompts, the J. Crew catalog, by restoring a textural reality that might as well be there (even if it is pure illusion), drives a final nail into the coffin of the fashion system, long before the fashion system even realized that it was being interred.

The New Age

In this respect, the J. Crew catalog is such a vanguard document that it seems absurd to label it avant-garde. It's just *garde*, ruthlessly promoting its own aesthetic, social, political, and economic program in terms of a purified dialect, as Mallarmé might have had it, of an archly conservative tribe. And, as Robert Hughes has rightly pointed out, most great advancements in the culture of art have been undertaken on the conservative watch. But unlike its companions in prospective cultural tyranny—Disney, Nike, Time Warner—J. Crew has the good sense to play it cool. Though its subliminal dictatorship of ease could not be finding grander success, the company has thus far resisted aggressive expansion into other lifestyle areas. There is no J. Crew Bath, no J. Crew Home, no J. Crew Scent. One senses that there might never be, even though the temptation is probably present.

It is as if J. Crew understands, somewhat like Microsoft, that all it needs to do is provide the theory plus a modicum of packaging—in this case, the clothes—leaving the more heavy-duty implementation of the J. Crew agenda up to the big lifters, like IKEA. In the same way that Microsoft requires no actual machines to run its insanely valuable code, J. Crew requires no physical correlative to its catalog, with the exception of a few retail outlets and, of course, the clothes. (Microsoft doesn't need to make computers, but it does need to deliver its code in boxes on disks, with some supporting documentation.) The point here is that the clothes are easy, just as the code is, to a degree, easy. The denial of the evident—that neither the desires manufactured by the J. Crew aesthetic nor the code written by Microsoft's programmers actually exists—is what's hard. To face consumers in exactly the opposite direction of common sense, in fact to convince them that common sense is less compelling than a

purely artificial set of experiences, indicates that the cure J. Crew offers will in all likelihood punish the competition, in the long run. At the very least, it will purchase the competition's complicity through imitation.

Never Surrender

Why then, if J. Crew is on the road to a fashion *fait accompli*, does the company endeavor so steadily to maintain a discriminating design sense? The glib maintenance of an ideology seems the readiest explanation that, and the sense that the company's employees and management want to have their cake and eat it, too: Crew wishes to control everything, but to do so without the visible expenditure of effort, to make it all look so very easy, so friendly and accessible. There's a strong Protestant work ethic at play here, the grim and unspoken sense that Crew has achieved its radical reworking of the American design ideology not through luck or real talent, or even grace, but through fundamental hard work. It is then classically American of this transcendence that J. Crew, in its vision of style and merchandizing, is innovative, self-made, and (on the dark flipside) perhaps more than a little scary, as all unified messianic visions must be.

Notes

1. J. Crew. 1996. "Eleventh hour reminder." *Christmas*, p. 24.
2. Ties and suits, in Crewland, merit closer investigation. J. Crew has for years maintained a men's haberdashery line that has only intermittently, and only in part, sold through the catalog, all the while maintaining the line at the stores. Men, it seems, are exceedingly reluctant to buy a suit through the mail. They appear to have trouble with mail-order ties, as well, though fewer qualms about shirts, shoes, and socks. Women, by contrast, will go for a mail-order suit. Since the suit, as Anne Hollander has pointed out, is the acid test of contemporary design—and perhaps modern fashion's crowning achievement—J. Crew's inability to integrate it into its aesthetic signifies a glaring chink in otherwise impenetrable armor. It is instructive to note, I think, that no one (not Giorgio Armani, not Calvin Klein, not Ralph Lauren, not Joseph Abboud, not Tommy Hilfiger) designing clothes for men has succeeded in disconnecting the suit from its history of heavy design. A suit is a suit, worn for a purpose, not to take a nap in. The temptation for Crew, clearly, is that men's haberdashery is lucrative (most good-quality suits ring up at more than $400, some substantially more) and represents an opportunity to score an ensemble sale of the sort that Banana Republic routinely manages with their suits. One explanation is that

American men, already unsteady about style, need to get a good look at what they're going to drop a stack of dollars on, need to *feel* the merchandise and get comfortable with the actual, rather than virtual, fit. Ties are another question. Crew's line of ties is, generally speaking, well designed and of high quality, and not priced too steeply. Neckwear, however, has been absent from recent catalogs *as a merchandise option*, while still functioning as a component of the overall catalog aesthetic.

3. Browne, Alix. 1996. "From main street to Prince Street." *Harper's Bazaar*. November, pp. 250–53, 267.
4. J. Crew. 1996. "Eleventh hour reminder." *Christmas*, p. 107.
5. Gandee, Charles. 1996. "The next best-dressed list." *Vogue*. December, p. 268.

Fashion Theory, Volume 1, Issue 3, pp.279–296
Reprints available directly from the Publishers.

Anti-Fashion: The 1970s[1]

Valerie Steele

"For the longest time everyone kept saying the Seventies hadn't started yet. There was no distinctive style for the decade, no flair, no slogans. The mistake we made was that we were all looking for something as startling as the Beatles, acid, Pop Art, hippies and radical politics. What actually set in was a painful and unexpected working-out of the terms the Sixties had so blithely tossed off." So observed Edmund White in his insightful essay, "Fantasia on the Seventies." White focused on the evolution of gay male sartorial style, away from early-1970s "fantasy clothes" and toward the "new brutalism" of Levis, leather and heavy work boots; but similar changes were occurring throughout the fashion culture.

Like the bastard child of the 1960s fashion revolution, 1970s style was in confused revolt against its progenitor. But because people disagreed about where fashion should go, it was pulled in radically different directions. People found this confusing, both at the time and in retrospect. In 1975, when Georgina Howell wrote her book, *In Vogue*, the last chapter was called "The Uncertain Seventies." In 1991, when she revised the book, she changed it to "The Schizophrenic Seventies."

Was it really "The Schizophrenic Seventies"? Or can we demonstrate that there was some deeper cultural unity beneath the chaotic clash of sartorial styles? To understand 1970s style, one must recognize that fashion was not in fashion. "Let us grant to the seventies its claim to antifashion, for the freedom to wear what you want, where and when you want, is finally here," declared journalist Clara Pierre in her 1976 book, *Looking Good: The Liberation of Fashion*. Hers was very much the opinion of the day, and the arbiters of fashion risked being dismissed as "fashion fascists" if they dared tell women what was "in" or "out." As a result, fashion journalists quickly adopted a new language of "freedom" and "choice."

The American journalist Tom Wolfe labeled the 1970s "The Me Decade," alluding to the narcissism and self-indulgence that seemed to characterize contemporary society. In an article entitled "The Sexed-Up, Doped-Up, Hedonistic Heaven of the Boom Boom '70s," published in *Harpers & Queen* (April 1980), Wolfe argued that people were mistaken in thinking of the 1970s as a period of calm after the "uproar" of the 1960s. Although the political radicalism of the student left had faded away after the end of the Vietnam War, in almost all other respects the cultural radicalism of the 1960s not only did not vanish, it diffused throughout the wider society. Both the drug culture and the sexual revolution, for example, became mass phenomena.

The Decade That Taste Forgot

If the hippies had one irrevocable effect on culture, including fashion, it was to destroy every rule, except the injunction to please oneself. Perhaps it is not surprising, then, that the 1970s have also been called "The Decade That Taste Forgot." Certainly, hot pants and platform shoes provide evidence that fashion's excesses were striking. It was a time of wide bellbottoms, wide lapels, and wide ties. But the defining characteristics of 1970s style were not limited to distortions of size. As the rules of taste and propriety were deliberately violated, the fashion system spawned crushed vinyl burgundy maxi-coats, avocado-green ultrasuede pants-suits, electric blue lycra "second-skin" bodystockings, and silver lurex halter tops. Polyester shirts were open to the waist, and dresses were slit up to the crotch.

Later in the century, when "Seventies style" was revived as Retro, it was this "trashy" aspect of the decade's fashions that received most attention. In March 1991, for example, American *Elle* began an article on "'70s Sound Style" (Pearlman 1991) by observing that "The early 1970s have a reputation for being deviant and nasty—which is one reason not to despise its current style revival." Were the 1970s really the "dark . . . hedonistic . . . underside of the sixties dream," as *Elle* put it? What was fashion really like in the 1970s?

I would argue that the fashions of the 1970s can be divided into two periods. From about 1970 through 1974, fashion was characterized by a continuation of many late-1960s themes, such as conspicuous outrageousness (epitomized by platform shoes and hot pants), retro fantasies (especially Edwardian and 1930s styles), and ethnic influences (notably Orientalism but also African-American styles). In its orientation toward youth, freedom, and other counterculture virtues like equality and anti-capitalism, the first phase of 1970s style might be described as late hippie diffusion.

From 1975 through 1979, however, fashion became simultaneously harsher and more conservative. On the level of street fashion, the peace and love ethos of the hippies was followed by the sex and violence of the punks. In the world of high fashion, a deliberately decadent style of "Terrorist Chic" dominated. Yet at the same time, middle-class people increasingly gravitated toward Dress-for-Success uniformity, which set the stage for the aggressive styles of the 1980s.

Hemlines Fall

When the 1970s began, however, the most striking development was the sound of hemlines falling. In January 1970, the Paris collections emphasized long skirts. Soon afterwards, a cartoon in *The New Yorker* showed two middle-aged businessmen wistfully staring at a couple of young women in the new leg-concealing styles: "It's the end of an era," sighed one of the men. Sixties style did not abruptly end in the first month of 1970, of course. Long dresses had already emerged among the hippies as early as 1967, and the fashion for maxi coats began in 1968. In 1969, the year of the so-called "micro mini," Marc Bohan was quoted as saying that since skirts could hardly get shorter, they would soon get longer. Nevertheless, the Paris collections did mark something of a turning-point.

After almost a decade of rapidly rising hemlines, the new, longer length made news around the world. Because the new hemline tended to fall at mid-calf, it was eventually dubbed the "midi," and there was considerable controversy over fashion's move from mini to midi. *Life* (anon. 1970) published a cover article on "The Great Hemline Hassle," featuring a two-page photo-spread of a woman's legs. "The latest word

is long," the magazine dutifully reported, "but . . . many women and all men hate to see the Mini go." Alongside a full-color photograph of a pretty young woman in a miniskirt was a large caption: "How can we bear to bid goodbye to all this?" Because the mini had been associated with youth and sexual liberation, it was said that the midi made women look old and ugly. The American designer Mollie Parnis insisted that "In this age of emphasis on sex and youth, no woman is going to add twenty years to her age by wearing skirts below her knees."

Because the midi was officially launched in Paris, the skirt-length debate was also interpreted in the United States in geopolitical terms: as French dictatorship versus American freedom. When Madame George Pompidou visited the United States, she naively told the press that Richard Nixon had admired her midi. Political humorist Art Buchwald joked that conservative Republican women had always worn midis. Yet the editor of *Women's Wear Daily*, which had promoted the midi quite aggressively, received an angry letter from a lady in Dallas, who wrote: "We love the miniskirt. And we support Nixon and Agnew too." Hatred of the midi made for strange political bedfellows. Liberals associated the mini with sexual liberation; but many conservatives were also pro-mini. According to Ellen Melinkoff's amusing social history *What We Wore* (1984), the Lieutenant Governor of Georgia (a very conservative Southern state) announced, "If any girl ever comes in with one of those midi things on, I'll have her kicked out of the Senate."

It is often said that hemlines reflect the state of the economy. Over the years, a number of journalists have theorized that hemlines go up in times of prosperity (such as the 1920s and 1960s) and go down when there is a recession or depression (as in the 1930s and 1970s). Although superficially plausible, this theory does *not* work. The stock market did fall in 1970 and again in 1973–4 with the oil crisis, but the market's ups and downs were not mirrored by a corresponding rise and fall of hemlines. Some of the hostility to the midi was economic in origin, however. Because the fall of the hemline coincided with the beginning of the deepest economic recession in years, many consumers were unable to invest in an entirely new wardrobe. Moreover, many manufacturers and retailers still had a considerable stock of miniskirts in the pipeline or inventory, with the result that they, too, protested against the new style.

If longer hemlines were not caused by a depressed economy, did they, perhaps, reflect women's changing role in society? Many feminists were critical of sexually explicit fashions, such as miniskirts, but they also rejected the way the fashion industry "manipulated" women's minds by promoting the new long skirts. Feminists' hostility to the very concept of changing fashion made them unlikely candidates as fashion trendsetters. Nevertheless, although feminism had little *direct* impact on the mini–midi controversy, the women's liberation movement was

an important phenomenon in the 1970s, which had an indirect influence on fashion.

The result of the great hemline controversy was, perhaps, inevitable. Hemlines fell. "They'll fight like hell, but they'll fall into line," predicted an anonymous expert who was quoted in the March 13, 1970 issue of *Life*. But it took another year or two before most women began to wear longer skirts. This delay has led many observers to conclude that the midi was a "flop," because women no longer "obeyed fashion's dictates." Despite its oversimplification, there is some truth in this argument. In the short run, the midi *was* a failure; the majority of women simply refused to buy it. More importantly, the hemline controversy showed that the fashion mood was anti-fashion and pro-choice. As fashion historian Marléne Delbourg-Delphis (1981) has observed, prior to 1963, women automatically followed fashion; during the 1960s, fashion shook people up, forcing them to accept fantastic styles; but in the 1970s public opinion rendered fashion "optional."

Public response to the mini–midi controversy was divided. A segment of the population wanted calm and realism; they gravitated towards a kind of uniformity, and ended by emphasizing hemlines that rested a little below the knee—or else they eschewed skirts entirely, in favor of trousers. For young women, fashion had a different trajectory, and the acceptance of longer skirts evolved out of the hippies' love of thrift-store clothes. Long crêpe gowns from the 1930s with tiny fabric-covered buttons were certainly not practical, but they were very romantic. Once these women became used to seeing longer skirts, the look spread rapidly. "For women who couldn't stand the midi one year, we sure bought a lot of granny dresses the next," recalls Melinkoff.

Although hemlines dropped, fashion continued to emphasize legs. Miniskirts might no longer be the height of fashion, but the new long skirts were often split from ankle to thigh. A 1970 evening dress by Saint Laurent, for example, opened in the front almost to the crotch. The appropriately named "hot pants" also appeared in Europe in 1970, spreading to America by early 1971, when they were featured in many fashion collections. Hot pants were essentially no more than very short shorts made from upscale fabrics such as velvet and silk. Because the style and even the name were popular with men, hot pants quickly became associated with prostitutes. But the style was also (briefly) worn even for weddings and in business offices. It was a short-lived fad, and only adopted by younger women, but while it lasted many hot pants were sold. Melinkoff quotes one woman, who recalled that one of her "favorite outfits was a pair of velour hot pants in royal purple with boots . . . to match, in purple suede."

Along with the kitschy pop creations that fashion historian Bruno du Roselle dubbed "savage styles," there was also a growing emphasis on conservative classics, or what the fashion press described as "real clothes for real people." Tired of fashion's excesses, yet sympathetic

to the hippies' creed of dressing to suit oneself, many people adopted a modernized version of the classics for work, and sportswear separates (especially jeans) for leisure. The situation was especially critical for working women, who adopted their own kind of anti-fashion. The 1970s was the era of women's liberation, and increasing numbers of women entered the higher echelons of the workforce. Disturbed by the hemline controversy, women increasingly chose to wear trousers, the traditional symbol of masculine power. In 1971, in France alone, the number of trousers for women sold jumped from eleven to fourteen million, while the number of dresses dropped from eighteen to fifteen million.

Bruno du Roselle (1973) has interpreted this development as part of "the return to calm." He admits that the idea of trousers for women had traditionally been one of fashion's strongest taboos, but nevertheless argues that incorporating trousers into a bourgeois uniform like the business suit effectively "annihilated" the revolutionary potential of trousers, while simultaneously "rejuvenating" the classic costume. I would argue, however, that the trouser suit or *tailleur-pantalon* was more radical than he thinks. The 1970s marked the first time in history that trousers were really accepted as female apparel, not only for informal occasions, but on the street and in the office—a development that really does seem to have reflected women's social and economic liberation.

A Return to Calm?

In any case, the very notion of a "return to calm" is problematic, since the mood of the 1970s was poised ambivalently between the revolutionary aspirations of the 1960s and the executive "power suits" of the 1980s. As Iain Finlayson wrote in *Denim: An American Legend* (1990): "Clothes could give the illusion that a person had 'dropped-out' a little bit." Finlayson quotes an advertising trade magazine that published an insightful essay on jeans in 1973: "Probably no single garment, outside of a religious order, has been so widely used as . . . a symbol for a change in lifestyle." Around the world from Haight Ashbury to Tokyo, jeans had been adopted as a symbol of youth and freedom. "What began as the hard-working garment of the hard-working man has been transmuted into the uniform of nonconformity—and a unisex uniform at that." But the uniform of a committed band of rebels and hippies soon spread to a much wider market. By the 1970s, blue jeans were no longer *really* the mark of the worker, the rebel, or the hippie, because everyone wore them. (In 1971 Levi Strauss received the Coty Fashion Critics Award, the "Oscar" of the American fashion industry.) Yet even as jeans became "co-opted" by the fashion system, their signifying value grew more powerful. "What was originally a

symbol of rebellion now becomes the symbol of continuity of that movement. As long as Levi's are around, nobody's copped out."

As the counterculture was being swallowed up by consumer society, "'real-life' denim became 'lifestyle' denim." Free to wear anything they wished, people overwhelmingly chose to wear jeans. But popular awareness of different brands and styles subverted the old utopian idea that everyone would be equal in identical jeans. Levi's and Wrangler's had to compete with a host of new "designer" blue jeans, produced by companies like Fiorucci, Gloria Vanderbilt, Pierre Cardin and Calvin Klein. The sex appeal of jeans was also increasingly emphasized. "Hustler" and "James Dean" became brand-names, to be followed in Italy by "Jesus Jeans." Successive blue jean fashions included bell-bottoms, hip-huggers, stovepipes, cuffed jeans, pleated and baggy jeans. Denim was stone-washed, dyed different colors, embroidered, and studded. In 1978, there was even a brief craze for see-through jeans.

Is it valid, though, to imply that jeans had once been "anti-fashion" before being co-opted by the fashion system? Many people have distinguished sharply between anti-fashion (or street style) and fashion. Ted Polhemus (1994), for example, insists that "The authenticity and sense of subcultural identity which is symbolized in streetstyle is lost when it becomes 'this year's fashion'—something which can be purchased and worn without reference to its original subcultural meaning." He argues that "Even within the fashion industry there is concern at what is seen as 'exploitation' of streetstyle creativity."

This argument is popular because it valorizes subcultural street styles and the people who wear them (marginal groups, workers, young people, minorities), while simultaneously attacking commercial fashion, on the grounds that it has a false and parasitic relationship to "authentic" anti-fashion. Obviously the fashion industry *has* often copied street style. Fashions no longer "trickle down," they usually "bubble up" from various subcultures. But contrary to what Polhemus believes, the creators of street style do not "naturally" evolve a pure and unchanging style, in contrast to fashion's artificial promotion of new, "trendy" fashions. There is a complex, dialectical relationship between fashion and anti-fashion.

Retro has frequently been criticized on the grounds that it represents either a loss of creativity on the part of fashion designers, or a perverse "nostalgia" for the past. Yves Saint Laurent's 1979–80 collection of 1940s-inspired fashions, for example, was savaged by journalists who failed to appreciate short skirts, wedge shoes, and a green fox-fur jacket with padded shoulders. It all seemed "vulgar," in "bad taste," "kitsch." Retro fashion evolved directly out of the hippies' pillaging of thrift stores, but its meaning constantly fluctuated. There was some interest among young people in rebellious 1950s youth styles, but probably the most popular period style was that of the 1930s. Visconti's film *The Damned* (which showed Ingrid Thulin vamping around as a fashionable Nazi)

became a cult favorite with fashion people. Films like *Cabaret* (1972) made the look of 1930s-style "decadence" available to a wider audience.

In retrospect, it seems clear that Retro is one of the most important stylistic features of postmodernism. The elements of pastiche and irony, the mixing together of different and often wildly clashing elements into a form of bricolage, is crucial to the late twentieth-century aesthetic sensibility. At first, however, it seemed closer to a 1960s counterculture philosophy.

In 1970 a group of young people in New York started a new fashion periodical called *Rags*, which featured examples of counterculture style, emphasizing cheap, vernacular garments, like denim jackets (ironically decorated with American flags), as well as older clothing culled from thrift shops. In line with the anti-consumerist hippie ideology, there were essays on how to tie-dye your clothes or hand-paint your platform shoes—although the magazine also praised a $50 shirt designed by the young designer Stephen Burrows. Rock star Mick Jagger was cited as a fashion trendsetter, and praised for a stage ensemble that consisted of a dog collar, scoop-necked T-shirt, nail-studded bell-bottoms, and a long tie-dyed silk scarf.

This last costume presaged two of the dominant trends of the 1970s: androgyny and punk. It also emphasized the continuing importance of music in youth fashion. In addition to rock and roll, the 1970s would see new kinds of music, like glam and glitter, heavy metal, funk (black party music), disco, and punk.

Glam rockers like David Bowie wore platform shoes, another major fad of the early 1970s. Isaac Hayes also allegedly owned 27 pairs of custom-made, skin-tight, thigh-high platform boots. Even ordinary mortals tottered along on platform shoes with two-inch soles and five-inch heels. Indeed, shoes and boots played an extremely important role in 1970s fashion, articulating various fashion philosophies. High fashion featured items like purple satin push-down evening boots and jodhpur boots in burgundy suede with reptile straps and heels. Latter-day hippies favored Frye boots worn with funky jeans or overalls, lumberjack shirts, and Army surplus socks. But most young urban blacks wouldn't have been caught dead in clothes like that. Instead they favored "funky chic" styles, such as boots with high heels and thick soles, Italian silk jerseys or black turtlenecks, tight pants that swelled out at the bottom (*not* jeans), and leather coats.

So-called "blaxploitation" films like *Shaft* (1971) and *Superfly* (1972) further popularized the style. The film *The Mack* portrayed a veritable fashion show of hustlers in crushed vinyl maxi coats, white fur wraps, and incredibly flared pants. Although older black people often complained about the implications of a look popularly associated with pimps and drugdealers, many young people responded positively to the combination of gangster style and black pride. Some years later, Ted Polhemus (1994) would point out that:

> the Pimp Look fits squarely and logically within that Dressing Up tradition . . . identified with . . . the Zooties . . . and others from socio-economically underprivileged situations. The early 1970s 'funkification' of this approach simply accentuated the blatantly erotic, in-your-face sexual possibilities of dress. For example, enormous flares in the trouser legs served to focus the eye on the contrasting ultra-tight fit around the crotch and bottom, while the use of expensive materials like suede and snakeskin underlined the Dressing Up, aspirational . . . message.

With black fashion in style, young black fashion designers like Stephen Burrows and Scott Barrie also achieved considerable success. Burrows, for example, had hardly graduated from the Fashion Institute of Technology when he acquired his own boutique. Famous for his body-conscious chiffon and jersey dresses, often with "lettuce-leaf" hems and almost always in brilliant colors, Burrows was one of five American designers to show at Versailles in 1973. His main influence came from African American popular dance. The 1970s also saw a continuation of the popularity of African clothes, like dashikis and headcloths, which resembled a more overtly politicized version of the wider interest in "ethnic" style. The Afro hairstyle, for example, became very popular.

The Punk "Style in Revolt"

Just as the mods and hippies had created their own styles of music and dress, so also did the punks. But instead of "peace and love," the punks created a deliberately aggressive, confrontational style, utilizing the visual accoutrements of sadomasochism. Their slogans were "Anarchy," "No Hope," and "We Are All Prostitutes." Like earlier youth rebels, they were anti-establishment and anti-bourgeois, but they were also specifically anti-"Leftover Hippies." The reason is not hard to find. As sociologist Fred Davis notes, "given the proximity of counterculture youth to mainstream middle-class society, it should not be surprising . . . that certain select hippie paraphernalia . . . [like jeans] had by the early 1970s come to be worn by adult middle-class men and women as well." The punks hated this, and they reserved their greatest scorn for aging rockers and veterans of 1968.

Punk was a deliberately "revolting style." Punk clothes were ripped, pierced with safety-pins, and decorated with swastikas, pornographic images, lavatory chains, and tampons. Even the bodies of the punks were pierced and shaved. As Dick Hebdidge writes in *Subculture: The Meaning of Style* (1979):

> Safety pins were . . . worn as gruesome ornaments through the cheek, ear or lip. "Cheap" trashy fabrics (plastic, lurex, etc.) in

> vulgar designs (e.g. mock leopard skin) and "nasty" colors, long discarded by the quality end of the fashion industry as obsolete kitsch, were salvaged by the punks and turned into garments . . . which offered self-conscious commentaries on the notions of modernity and taste . . . In particular, the illicit iconography of sexual fetishism was . . . exhumed from the boudoir, closet and the pornographic film and placed on the street.

The punk style was initially greeted with horror. Yet within a very short time, it was a major influence on international fashion. For just as the hippies' affinity with exotic and "retro" styles had provided a source of inspiration for mainstream fashion designers, so did the fashion world respond to the punks' obsession with the taboo realm where sex and violence meet. Vivienne Westwood, in particular, enthusiastically embraced punk, and her role underscores the *naïvêté* of any rigid separation between anti-fashion and fashion. In 1971, with mainstream fashion divided between mass-market neo-hippie looks and incipient neoconservatism, Westwood opened a 1950s revival shop in London, evoking the rebels of an earlier era. By the mid-1970s the store had been transformed into a punk/fetish shop called Sex, where Westwood catered to a mixed clientele of about half "genuine" sexual fetishists and half young people who wanted to look "bad." She designed and wore rubber and leather bondage outfits, "cruel" shoes, and other extreme fashions.

Few other fashion designers went as far as Westwood in incorporating the most offensive and threatening elements of punk style. Only Westwood had the nerve to print T-shirts emblazoned with swastikas and pornographic pictures, for example. But "ripped" garments decorated with safety-pins soon appeared in the collections of other fashion designers like Zandra Rhodes, from which the style filtered down to the mass market. Punk is a prime example of the new brutalism that characterized the entire fashion system during the later 1970s. It is important to stress, however, that the sinister undercurrent of violence and sexual "perversity" was not limited to subcultural styles.

1970s fashion, in general, was heavily influenced by what one American scholar (Selzer 1979) described as "Terrorist Chic." Black leather became stylish, precisely because it evoked images of sadomasochistic sex, which was regarded as "the last taboo." Pornographic movies like *Angelique in Black Leather* and the homoerotic *Nights in Black Leather* contributed to the mystique, as did art films like *Maitresse*, which was about a dominatrix, and featured fetish costumes in leather and rubber by Karl Lagerfeld. Even department store windows featured mannequins that were blindfolded, tied up, and shot. Fashion photography, in particular, was implicated in the new style.

The House of Dior hired Chris von Wangenheim to photograph its costume jewelry, resulting in a famous advertisement that showed a

Figure 1
Halston brown suede coordinates including hot pants, shirt, belt, and fur trimmed maxi coat, 1971. The Museum of F.I.T. gift of Mrs Michawl Kaiser, 88.29.39. Photograph by Irving Solero

woman with her wrist in the jaws of a fierce-looking attack dog. Other top fashion photographers, like Guy Bourdin and Helmut Newton, posed models in scenarios that critics described as violent and "pornographic." Because of the puritanism of American society, there was a real scandal when in 1975 *Vogue* published a photo-essay by Helmut Newton called "The Story of Oh-h-h," which showed a woman hungrily eyeing a man's half-naked body, and another woman smiling as a man unfastened the top of her bikini. French *Vogue* permitted much more overt eroticism, but even in France there were complaints when Newton posed Jenny Capitain as a "cripple" in a picture that strongly resembled fetishistic pornography.

"Cabaret freaks and perverse sex find echoes in today's decadence," wrote art critic Barbara Rose in an essay on "The Beautiful and the Damned" published in American *Vogue* (November 1978). According to Rose, Newton's "photographs of beautiful women trapped or constricted accentuate the interface between liberation and bondage . . . An anonymous hotel room evokes fantasies of potential erotic adventure. Glittering surfaces catch and reflect light in images that couple elegance with pain, fin-de-siècle opulence with contemporary alienation." Yet because there were usually "no visible oppressors" in these sado-masochistic "mini-dramas," the photographs implied that the "bondage was of woman's own making."

Newton was hired as a consultant for the horror film *The Eyes of Laura Mars*, which depicted Faye Dunaway as a fashion photographer whose work mixed sex and violence. The film not only publicized some of Newton's most infamous pictures, it also staged typically Newton-esque fashion shoots. In one scene, for example, two models wearing nothing but underwear, high heels and fur coats engage in a violent hair-pulling catfight in front of a burning car. "You don't have to pull so hard," complains one of the women (played by a real model), but the photographer encourages even greater violence. In another scene, while disco music blares, a model pretends to shoot a male model, who lies "dead" and bloodied in a pool of water at her feet.

If Newton's pictures frequently focused on sexual aggression, often positioning women as the aggressors, the work of Guy Bourdin focused explicitly on the connections between sex and death. Already in the 1960s Bourdin had posed an elegant fashion model in front of the bloody carcasses hanging in a butcher's shop. In the 1970s he created even more controversial images. His shoe advertisements for Charles Jourdain were especially notorious. In one advertisement he depicted what appeared to be the aftermath of a fatal car crash; one of the victim's shoes lay at the side of the road. Bourdin also shot a notorious lingerie catalog for Bloomingdale's department store. Most lingerie photographs depict a single conventionally attractive female, posed in a romantic private setting, and lit naturalistically. But Bourdain posed several "whorish" women together in settings that resembled brothels, and he photo-

Figure 2
Stephen Burrows calf-length A-line dress in wool double knit, Fall 1970. The Museum of F.I.T., gift of Stephen Burrows, 92.105. Photograph by Irving Solero

graphed them using an intrusive hard-flash, which called attention to the presence of the photographer. As a result the pictures looked like hard-core pornography or police photography.

Although this type of photography has frequently been attacked as misogynistic, some feminists defend it against charges of sexism, on the grounds that it is "subversive" and "liberating," because it makes explicit the subtexts that are latent in other fashion images: themes like narcissism, lesbianism, and the male gaze. In this respect the "decadent" style of 1970s fashion photography may be compared with punk fashion, for punk also presents images of "bad girls" in stilettos and fishnet stockings, subversively appropriating the symbols of prostitution and sexual perversion, and implicitly refusing to accept the division of women into sexless Madonnas and sexual Whores.

Rich Peasants

Despite the punk explosion in London, Paris soon regained its position as the capital of fashion. Yves Saint Laurent, in particular, put his mark on the decade, and his career throws much light on the evolution of fashion. Aware that his couture prices were "prohibitive" for many women, Saint Laurent told French *Elle* in 1971 (Anon. 1971) that henceforth he was going to focus on ready-to-wear, because his "true public" consisted of "young women . . . who work." A striking picture published in *Elle* showed one of his couture dresses costing 5,500 francs next to a remarkably similar ready-to-wear dress retailing at 650 francs. If he did not close his couture house, he explained, it was "because I cannot morally throw 150 people on the pavement. I guard my private clients for my workers, and not the other way round." Haute couture, he argued, "perhaps will last another five or ten years. Not more."

Later he would reassess the situation, and conclude that the luxury and fantasy of the couture played a vital creative role in society. Although he was famous for his trouser suits, his evening clothes often revelled in the "retro" and "ethnic" influences so beloved of the hippies. With his Russian—or Ballets Russes—collection of 1976–7 Saint Laurent launched a phantasmagoria of Oriental influences. Building on the big look of the mid-1970s, he created spectacularly luxurious costumes, such as sable-trimmed gold brocade Cossack coats and long gypsy skirts in iridescent silks. Some observers complained that the collection was "nostalgic" and too close to "costume" to be really wearable, and leftists characterized it as his "rich peasant" collection; but it triggered a new wave of ethnic fashions, which were produced at all price points.

Then in the winter of 1977–8 Saint Laurent produced his Chinese collection, featuring yet more theatrical luxury. The romanticization of the Orient has, of course, a long history in the West. But the popularity of the "Chinese Look" in the 1970s was especially significant.

Partly the result of the growing normalization of relations between the People's Republic of China and the Western democracies, the new Orientalism embraced both Chinese work clothes and golden brocades. The work clothes had as one subtext an enthusiasm for leftist, anti-colonial politics and a new Western fantasy about the workers' paradise. By contrast, the "Mandarin look" reflected melodramatic fantasies about ancient, faraway *Cathay*. In 1980 Saint Laurent launched his new perfume, Opium.

But just as Pop Art had been replaced by Minimalism in the world of the fine arts, so also did fashion minimalism flourish. The American designer Halston was especially influencial. He created soft, relatively unconstructed, interrelated separates. He focused, in particular, on trousers and tunics for both day and evening. He loved using the new and expensive artificial fiber Ultrasuede, and was also known for his liquid jersey—so appropriate for the "soft seventies." Yet for all the elegant minimalism of Halston's style, the new brutalism was also apparent in the window displays created for him by Victor Hugo, such as the one showing a roll of silk charmeuse—with a black leather whip tossed on to it.

Thus, along with terrorist chic, the second half of the 1970s saw a growing emphasis on what might be called "conservatism with a choice." In practice, this meant slightly-below-the-knee skirts, trousers, and "dress-for-success" suits. These clothes were often shown on healthy-looking fashion models, like Lauren Hutton, who were made-up to look "natural" in sheer lip gloss and other minimalist cosmetics. But it was also possible to style and photograph even conservative-looking clothes with a decadent edge, through the use of glamorous make-up, fetishist accessories, and hard-flash photography. The "no make-up" look of the early-to-mid 1970s was increasingly replaced by a look of deliberately

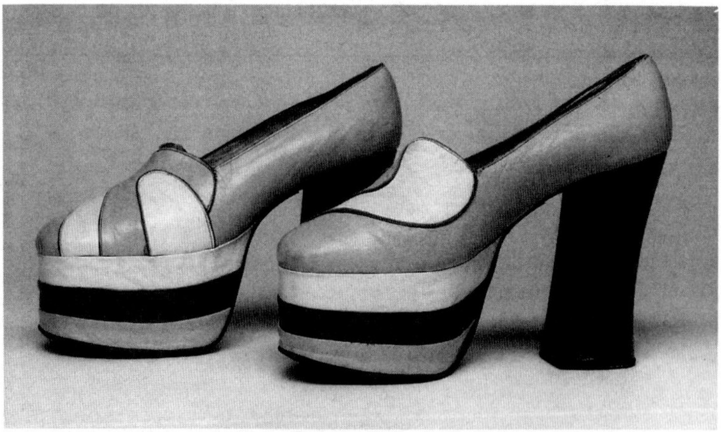

Figure 3
Platform shoes by Greca, 1970–2. The Museum of F.I.T., Museum Purchase, P29.11.9. Photograph by Irving Solero

heightened artificiality. Like vampires, fashion models had pale, pale skin and deep red lips. Indeed, lips were the most important facial feature, in contrast to the previous period, when the eyes were emphasized. Now that doe-eyed look was dead, replaced by a shiny, wet, blood-red mouth.

Note

1. Excerpted from *Fifty Years of Fashion: New Look to Now*, New Haven: Yale University Press.

References

Anón. 1970. "The Great Hemline Hassle." *Life*, 13 March 1970.

Anon. 1971. "YSL choisit le prêt à porter." *Elle*, 9 June 1971.

Delbourg-Delphis, Marléne. 1981. *Le Chic et le Look: Histoire de la mode féminine et des moeurs de 1850 à nos jours*. Paris: Hachette.

Finlayson, Iain. 1990. *Denim: An American Legend*. New York: Simon & Schuster.

Hebdidge, Dick. 1979. *Subculture: The Meaning of Style*. New York: Methuen.

Howell, Georgina. 1975. *In Vogue: Six Decades of Fashion*. London: Allen Lane.

Howell, Georgina. 1991. *In Vogue: Seventy-Five Years of Style*. London: Condé Nast Books.

Melinkoff, Ellen. 1984. *What We Wore: An Off-Beat Social History of Women's Clothing*. New York: Quill.

Pearlman, Jill. 1996. "'70s Sound Style." *Elle*, March 1991.

Pierre, Clara. 1976. *Looking Good: The Liberation of Fashion*. New York: Readers Digest Books.

Polhemus, Ted. 1994. *Streetstyle: From Sidewalk to Catwalk*. London: Thames and Hudson.

Rose, Barbara. 1978. "The Beautiful and the Damned." *Vogue*, November 1978.

Roselle, Bruno du. 1973. *La Mode*. Paris: Imprimerie Nationale.

Selzer, Michael. 1979. *Terrorist Chic: An Exploration of Violence in the Seventies*. New York: Hawthorn Books.

White, Edmund. 1994. "Fantasia on the Seventies," in *The Burning Library*, ed. David Bergman. New York: Knopf.

Wolfe, Tom. 1980. "The Sexed-Up, Doped-Up, Hedonistic Heaven of the Boom Boom '70s," *Harpers & Queen*, April 1980.

Figure 4
Halston tailored shirt dress in beige ultrasuede, 1972. The Museum of F.I.T., gift of Mrs. Sidney Merians, 82.193.4. Photograph by Irving Solero

Fashion Theory, Volume 1, Issue 3, pp.297–312
Reprints available directly from the Publishers.
Photocopying permitted by licence only.

New Directions: Fashion History Studies and Research in North America and England

Alexandra Palmer

Alexandra Palmer is the Nora E. Vaughan Fashion Costume Curator at the Royal Ontario Museum, Toronto, Canada. Her doctoral work was on haute couture in Toronto during the 1950s.

The great voids in fashion scholarship can be partially explained by the fact that the study of dress often carries with it negative associations. One scholar, for example, recently described the field as:

> a prolonged picnic attended by hordes of schoolchildren and enthusiastic girls on textile or design courses undertaking 'projects.' The work of scholars approaching the history of dress from the point of view of the history of art or the history of material culture—and the last generation has seen important developments in these approaches—has not been integrated into economic or social history. (Harte 1991)

This comment, while sexist, nonetheless acknowledges that there have been important developments, and it is indeed true that the traditional study of dress history has largely been based upon old art-historical methods of stylistic analysis. One of the central reasons for this is because many of the first studies came from those working in museums, and the basic training was often art-historical.

The fact remains that the serious study of dress does continue to have loaded associations with Harte's "enthusiastic girls." A contributing factor is that there is little formal academic training that addresses fashion or costume history. Fashion has constantly been faced with what Jacqueline Beaudoin-Ross and Pamela Blackstock have called "a fight to achieve recognition as a valid area of study" (1991: 42). Like many other academics who are currently teaching fashion courses, my path through the labyrinth of higher educational institutions only appears fairly straightforward. I have a BA in Art History from the University of Toronto (1979), an MA in Costume and Textiles from New York University (1981), and a PhD from the University of Brighton (1995).

In England, fashion history may be taught at an undergraduate level as part of design history programs that often include industrial design. In North America design history itself is not part of any undergraduate pedagogy. Where it does exist it tends to be found in curricula centered on the practice of a design discipline, such as architecture, graphic design, or fashion design. It is rarely found in a purely academic program, and, when it is, is most likely to be an elective course within an art history program. The situation at graduate level is marginally better. The MA in The History of Decorative Arts offered at The Bard Graduate Center, like the MA in Museum Studies at the Fashion Institute of Technology, offers only a few courses on fashion and textiles.

Within North America, the only MA program that concentrates solely on the study of costume and textiles is the program at New York University offered in conjunction with the Costume Institute of the Metropolitan Museum of Art. All the six costume classes are taught by a single instructor—a fact which limits diverse viewpoints. The syllabus requires a final project but not a formal thesis. This restriction makes this chiefly a terminal degree, yet the reality is that a doctorate is a basic requirement for both academic and more and more museum positions. Another difficulty is that, given the lack of undergraduate training, much of the time spent in graduate studies can focus on teaching basics, such as the development of styles.

The greatest concentration of fashion and history-related courses tend to be situated within Home Economics (more currently, "Human Ecology") departments of universities scattered across North America. Many of these programs house interesting costume collections that are used for teaching and research. Each has its own strengths and has developed out of the late-nineteenth-century philosophy that teaching and professionalizing homemaking skills, such as sewing, raised women's

status. A few of those better known for producing fashion historians are the University of Minnesota, the University of Alberta, the University of Rhode Island and Ohio State University. However, these programs often focus on teaching a "scientific" analytical methodology that tends to concentrate on quantitative analysis without incorporating a broader cultural framework. A serious problem with this approach is that it usually fails to contextualize findings, thereby leaving one wondering what to do with the results, how to apply them to other research, and how they critically or culturally inform either artefacts and our understanding of their use and function, or socio-cultural history. The "scientific method" obliterates any of the nuances and personal or cultural perspectives of production, consumption and taste that make fashion such a complex and engrossing study.

Opportunities for specifically studying the history of costume are more formalized in England. The Courtauld History of Dress MA at the University of London is probably the most famous. This program is based on a classical art-historical model. More recently Winchester School of Art, now amalgamated with the University of Southampton, offers an MA in dress and textile history and also accepts PhD students. Graduate studies at the MA and PhD levels can also be taken at the Royal College of Art, and at the University of Brighton; the latter two are offered under the broader umbrella of design history programs. It is these limited opportunities for study that compound and help to explain why there is so very little theoretical and formal underpinning to such a rich discipline. This issue has been recently explored by Finkelstein in *After A Fashion* (1996).

However, recent important scholarly developments and escalating interest in costume from other disciplines demonstrate that it is imperative for traditional fashion historians to apply a more critical, theoretical and analytical methodology in their research. For the most part, fashion historians have not yet begun to integrate broader theoretical models into their work. This situation is nowhere more pronounced than in studies of the modern period, particularly when the focus has been on designers or couturiers. Here the field is still informed by the traditional view of fashion designers as great artists, with little or no reference to their work in relation to patterns of consumption and larger global structures.

There are a few exceptions. Anne Coleman has examined, in a historical, social and commercial context, the diffusion of the work of a single couturier—Worth—in the late nineteenth and early twentieth centuries (1989, 1990). Her research documents and analyzes couture as a product, though it does not discuss prices, labor or the financial structure of the house. Her other work on nineteenth- and twentieth-century Paris couturiers Doucet and Pingat has also enriched the understanding of these individuals beyond that of the couturier as "artist" (1989). Writings by Dominique Veillon (1990) on the production

of French fashion during the Second World War and by Lou Taylor (1992) have begun to unpack some of the myths surrounding the couture structure and individual designers at this time. Melissa Leventon's essay on couture in America looks at the impact of European couture in a North American context and outlines the role of American merchants (1989). And Lesley Miller's book *Balenciaga* also moves beyond the standard format and discusses not only the structure of the house but also the marketing and the aftermath. The more recent exhibition catalogue on Jacques Fath by Valérie Guillaume (1993) also marks a very positive leap forward, as it embraces issues of couture licencing and production and a detailed examination of the couture house operations, as well as details about the couturier himself.

In addition, there is an increasing number of analytic studies by social and economic historians primarily using seventeenth- and eighteenth-century dress as a source of social and economic history that more clearly reflect the latest academic trends. These authors include Daniel Roche (1989), John Styles (1993), Beverly Lemire (1990, 1991), Laurel Thatcher Ulrich (1991), Michael Sonenscher (1987), and Lorna Weatherill (1988). There are also new works by scholars working in seemingly unrelated disciplines, such as *Men in Black* by John Harvey, a literary historian, and *The Empire of Fashion* by Gilles Lipovetsky, a philosopher.

Another school of dress history scholarship has emerged over the last few years from (post-)feminist theorists. Caroline Evans and Minna Thornton, for example, state that they do "not analyse fashion in terms of particular political issues, economics or sociology . . ."; rather, they address "fashion as a discourse which is culturally marginalized within the hierarchies of art and of history" (1989: xiv–xv). Coming from art history, they wish to step out of the art history mold and loosely follow the style of semiotician Roland Barthes (1983). Other feminist writers, such as sociologist Elizabeth Wilson (1985), have greatly contributed to the critical discourse by analyzing the political and cultural implications of dress. However, as none of these authors is grounded in dress history, their research is not object-based and they may generalize or even introduce errors about the actual clothing.

American dress historian, Valerie Steele (1996, 1991, 1988, 1985), continues to analyze fashion from a base that combines historical and cultural analysis with feminist, postmodern and critical theory, though she has not yet seriously drawn upon material culture to support her work. By contrast, Rozsika Parker in *The Subversive Stitch. Embroidery and the Making of the Feminine* (1989), is one of the few historians who does combine art-historical research and material culture analysis with theories on gender and women's history. Christopher Breward (1995) brings contemporary theory, gender studies and cultural analysis to his work, though to date I am unaware of his having worked with material culture.

Many of these studies tend to be based on an interest in the development of consumption and industrial production, social mobility, or gender and class structures. Documentary data on dress are taken from a range of archival texts, inventories and wills to substantiate the authors' theories, despite the fact that the kinds of clothing and textiles featured in their research are often extant in museum collections. Few are written by dress historians and none uses object analysis to support or inform the history. Material culture images are sometimes included to "illustrate" the text, but rarely to inform it. For example Beverly Lemire's 1990 article in the spring issue of *Material History Bulletin*, an issue dedicated to the theme of textiles and manufacture, uses material culture images to enhance the text, but does not actually make direct reference to any individual examples.

However, Laurel Thatcher Ulrich (1991), Beverly Lemire (1994 paper) and Jill Fields (1997) have begun to integrate material culture into their work. Yet, in general, material culture tends to be overlooked by those pursuing the latest theoretical writings and social studies, even though linking documentary data to material culture is an under-utilized and rewarding academic tool. This was pointed out by Joan Thirsk (1990), who argued for the use of material culture in conjunction with other research methods and illustrated her argument with a discussion of the work of Heita Kawakatsu. Drawing on material culture, Kawakatsu identified various qualities of sixteenth- to eighteenth-century cottons exported to Asia, and demonstrated that "cottons made in England and India were not, in fact, in direct competition with each other; they were satisfying different consumer groups with different tastes and different purses." (Thirsk: 45) This analysis may have been implied or suspected by historians, but the material culture evidence has proved this beyond any doubt, and is now central to further scholarship in this area.

But as Daniel Miller has written, "There is at present no academic discipline which sees it as its specific project to examine the nature of artifacts as cultural forms" (1987: 110). Further, the issue of how to use material culture analysis has recently divided scholars and raised questions concerning the appropriate methodology for the study of dress and design history. Nancy Rexford classifies dress scholars into three groups: "Connoisseur," which she defines as "someone concerned with beauty"; "Antiquarian," or "a scholar who accepts all objects as having value because each one contributes to a balanced and comprehensive understanding of the past"; and "Historian," the one "who sees his essential function as interpreting the past" (1988: 69). Her classification system supplies no suggestions for integration or further inquiry. (Her own work would be classified as Antiquarian.) What she is in fact championing is the need to use material culture. Such an approach is also favored by Joan Severa and Merrill Horswill, who state that ". . . the costume artifact, when subjected to formal analysis, may be expected

to reveal evidence of attitudes, belief systems and assumptions which shed light upon a culture" (1989: 53).

But why has this not been done by most fashion historians? Clearly, to do so requires moving beyond the object itself and inquiring into its social and cultural setting and function. This demands employing a multidisciplinary methodology that many dress historians seem unwilling to adopt.

Fashion historian Patricia Cunningham argues for this approach, and says that ". . . we should let artifacts speak for themselves and not be drawn into following formulas and set strategies" (1988: 77). Yet artefacts do not "speak"; rather, interpretation and meaning are supplied through the use of structured methodologies. Cunningham suggests that fashion historians have to "let our own questions and materials lead us to new approaches . . . we must devise our own models" (p. 77). In particular she urges those working on the twentieth century to "try to discover what clothing meant to wearers and observers" (p. 78). She suggests looking at the fields of art history, sociology, psychology, economics, women's studies, American studies and popular culture studies, as well as others.

It is quickly apparent that the main problem of using a multidisciplinary methodology is knowing what research areas to draw upon, as the range of available disciplines can be overwhelming and endless. Additionally, there is the potential problem of reconciling object study and documentary references. This problem was addressed by Adrienne Hood in reference to textile history, and she suggested collaborating with scholars from other disciplines (1990: 8). Analysis of artefacts does naturally lead into other research areas prompted by the object itself: "analysis of artefacts must begin with the most obvious characteristic . . . This factor may provide the key to understanding its power and significance in cultural construction" (D. Miller 1987, 98–9).

A methodology for costume study is, I feel, at its best when it is multidisciplinary and includes material culture analysis. This enables scholars to contextualize artefacts and documents in a multi-layered fashion. When possible, a material culture analysis can be drawn from the personal biographies imbedded in the clothes and supplemented with the oral histories of those who designed, made, modeled, sold, bought and wore them. These histories can then be amplified by archival research, both documentary and visual, as well as by contemporary newspaper and magazine reports, and current academic scholarship and theory from any one of a number of fields, including design and social or cultural history, economic history and gender studies. Employing a multidisciplinary methodology is particularly appropriate for investigating the modern period, which is often recorded in numerous and varied media. By integrating multiple facets of the subject from a range of sources one can overcome the prejudice imposed by the limits of the evidence in each research area.

For my own research on couture worn in Toronto in the postwar years, a multidisciplinary methodology was developed in order to be able to debate all the issues raised, from the design house through to the distributor and the consumer. I encountered little problem in reconciling object analysis and research data, as each history greatly informed the other, suggesting a natural marriage. The artefact supported the history, and theory was deduced from the objects themselves—rather than, as commonly happens, the object being selected to support a theory. While employing an economic analysis, the study focused on dress history within the larger contexts of design and cultural history and Canadian women's social history. These areas were all wedded with oral history research, and the entire body of work propelled by object analysis in an attempt to reveal the many meanings of the objects through tracing their individual and collective biographies. Over three hundred objects were examined in order to capture both the individual and the collective picture. Through a few sample case studies I will illustrate the validity of employing a multidisciplinary methodology that is based on material culture.

My detailed examination of couture garments raised many questions. Labels themselves suggested several avenues of inquiry, including undocumented designers such as the American couturier, Oldric Royce. Labels also hinted at various patterns of consumption. One read, *Christian Dior, UK, Holt Renfrew*. How did the meaning and origins of this differ from another that read *Christian Dior Original, in Canada Exclusive with Holt Renfrew & Co. Limited*? Bond tags left on many Canadian worn examples testified to certain trading patterns, while the designs and designers represented in private and museum collections also gave actual evidence of purchase and wear that could not be obtained from fashion magazines and advertisements.

The amount of wear and numbers of alterations on so much couture absolutely contradicted notions of conspicuous consumption, and suggested that owners, even the most wealthy women, placed a high social value on couture.

Case Study #1: Schiaparelli evening dress

Material Culture Evidence

A pale pink silk faille Schiaparelli evening dress was donated and worn by a prominent Torontonian, Lady Eaton [Figure 1, ROM 956.178.4]. The shirring is caught with an inside tape that reads "Schiaparelli," confirming the designer. There were no alterations in the large-size dress, which indicated that Lady Eaton ordered it at the couture house in Paris. She is known to have patronized this house.

ROYAL
FORM

Documentary Research

The Schiaparelli design sketch located in Paris (UFAC D73-21-3992) confirmed the date of spring 1949 and also shows the design with a hooded red velvet shoulder cape that is not part of the ROM piece. Further archival research uncovered a society photograph published in the Canadian magazine *Mayfair* (Jan. 1950, p. 21). It depicts Lady Eaton wearing the dress the previous November to the Royal Winter Fair equestrian event, which was a key social function within the Toronto social season. Additional research also uncovered a *Globe and Mail* (17 Nov. 1951, p. 12) newspaper description of Lady Eaton wearing the dress a year later to the Hunt Club Ball. Here it was described as "a white taffeta gown . . . shirred with short puffed sleeves, the wide skirt caught up in tiny scallops. With it she wore a diamond tiara and pearl and diamond necklace."

Conclusion

The notion that rich women rarely appeared in the same dress twice is refuted by the fact that Lady Eaton was not afraid of being seen in the same dress by the same social group on at least two occasions. Further, a spring design was considered suitable for the winter season, thus dispelling the notion of the seasonal importance placed upon fashions by the fashion-makers and press. This probably applies more strongly to evening dresses, as this example demonstrates.

The dress was given to the ROM in 1956. Thus it had the potential to be worn for seven years, and thus documented my argument that the investment in couture was viewed as long-term, and its value was derived from the fact that the design would "last" for several years; and in this case across seasons. This was substantiated by the 1951 press report of her 1949 design.

Case Study #2: Balenciaga Cocktail Dress. Second-hand couture

Material culture led me into unforeseen directions such as Toronto's second-hand couture trade, where couture was largely sold in the Junior League Opportunity Shop, the annual Toronto Symphony Sale, the annual Hadassah Bazaar, and the first commercial establishment, Shoppe d'Or, dealing in high-quality or so called "gently used" clothing.

Figure 1
Schiaparelli evening dress of pale pink silk faille. Purchased at the couture house in spring 1949 and worn for several years. ROM 956.178.4 (Photography Brian Boyle)

Material Culture Evidence

A Balenciaga dress in the ROM collection was dated c.1958 [Figure 2 ROM 987.153.1]. The dress was hemmed up about 4 inches in both the sheath and in the wide bias-cut floating back panel. No material had been cut away to facilitate the hemming up. The shorter length was typical of the late 1950s fashion.

WOLF
FORM CO.
N.Y.C.

Documentary Research

Photographic archival records at Balenciaga recorded the design was earlier than cataloged, as it dated from the Fall 1948 collection. Further, it appeared in a color sketch in *Vogue* (1 Oct. 1948, p. 156) drawn by Eric, as well as in *L'Officiel* (Oct. 1948, p. 71).

Oral History

The dress came into the collection with information from the Canadian donor, who said she had purchased it in a second-hand resale shop in New York City.

Conclusion

As the dress was purchased second-hand in the USA, one can surmise that it was either purchased at the design house by an American client or else imported by an American retailer. The fact that it has no interior alterations in the seams may indicate the former.

However, ten years after its design it was purchased by a Canadian and worn in Canada. Thus the design was appropriate for both cultural tastes. The design was worn and in use for a minimum of ten years by two owners, 1948–58, yet was finally given up in 1987, when it was donated to the museum.

Thus the initial investment in couture is further substantiated by its second-hand monetary and social value. This second-hand couture market is an area that is totally undocumented, yet continues historical clothing traditions of bequeathing and trading in clothing which have real economic and cultural value. The fact that the dress had been updated only by carefully hemming it, with no loss, not only testifies to the longevity of couture design, but also continues the tradition of altering valuable and respected garments in such as way as to be able to "undo" the alterations and retain as much of the original design and fabric as possible for future wear.

Case Study #3: Bonded Models

Figure 2
Balenciaga cocktail dress of black silk taffeta, fall 1948. Purchased second-hand in New York City during the mid-1950s. ROM 987.153.1 (Photography Brian Boyle)

Bonded models were another form of "gently used" couture for Canadians. This was an area of great importance, as Canada was an unloading ground for New York stores and manufacturers that imported original European models in bond to avoid duty. The garments were used in fashion shows, for copying and adaptations; but all had to be exported within three to six months. Canadian retailers and couture customers profited from this somewhat unusual trade.

Material Culture Evidence

Many bonded models were sold to Canada and South America—some still with bond tags in place [Figures 3 and 4a, b, ROM 970.286.ab].

WOLF
FORM CO.
N.Y.C.

One dress from the English design house of Norman Hartnell reads, "Bergdorf Goodman item #2801." On the reverse, "N.Y. Int'l Airport 1 year in bond."

Oral History

An interview with Ollie Smythe, the buyer for Eaton's department store in Toronto, revealed that obtaining bonded models was a competitive business between high-end Toronto retailers. Eaton's was losing the competition, so Smythe was sent to New York City to buy as many bonded models as she could. She bought from stores and manufacturers whatever was available. There was no selection process, as a flat rate was paid per item.

An interview held with Andrew Goodman of Bergdorf Goodman in New York City revealed that Bergdorf's alone imported 80–100 bonded models each season. This one source suggested larger numbers in trade. Further interviews with Toronto customers who purchased bonded models revealed the trade and meaning of these clothes. These were re-sold in Toronto, and stores fought to get them, as did clients. Favored clients were called to try them on. They knew that the competition was fierce and so would immediately go to the stores, as the choice was available to whomever came first.

Conclusion

Bonded models are a key to investigating differences between North American and European taste, as well as an important link in the complex area of trade and couture licencing during the 1950s. The European couture industry relied upon North American commercial clients, who purchased the bulk of couture production as samples and bonded models. This simultaneously undermined the exclusivity and prestige of haute couture while also sustaining it.

Summary

Through these case studies I hope to have demonstrated the significance of researching costume from multiple areas, and the importance of including material culture in a methodology. Object analysis is also often the strength of many traditional costume historians, who have a great deal of knowledge, understanding and ability to interpret artefacts. However, material culture analysis has to be set within a broader academic framework and not just be for its own sake. Liaison with scholars in other areas should be encouraged, as it is through cross-disciplinary interaction that more dynamic research can be suggested and pursued.

Figure 3
Hartnell cocktail dress of taupe satin and velvet with silver sequins, 1950s. Purchased by Bergdorf Goodman in bond and resold to Simpsons department store in Toronto. ROM. 970.286.ab (Photography Brian Boyle)

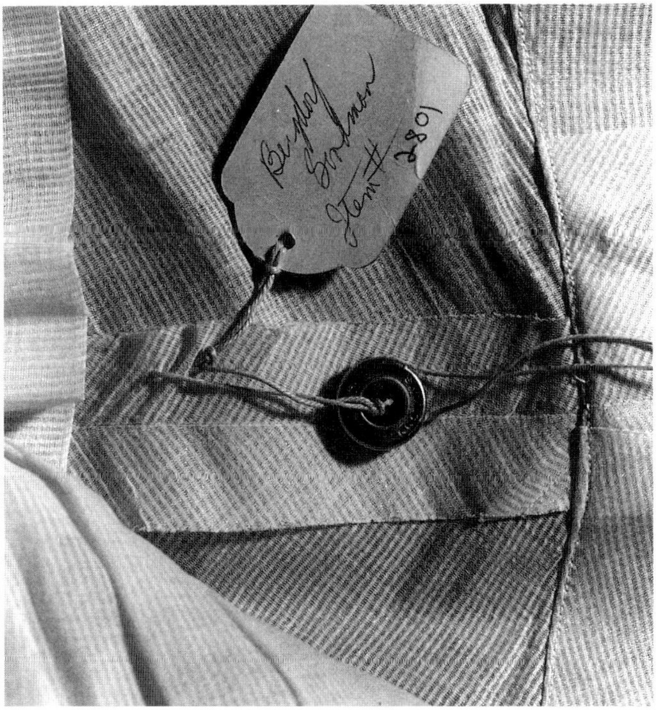

(a)

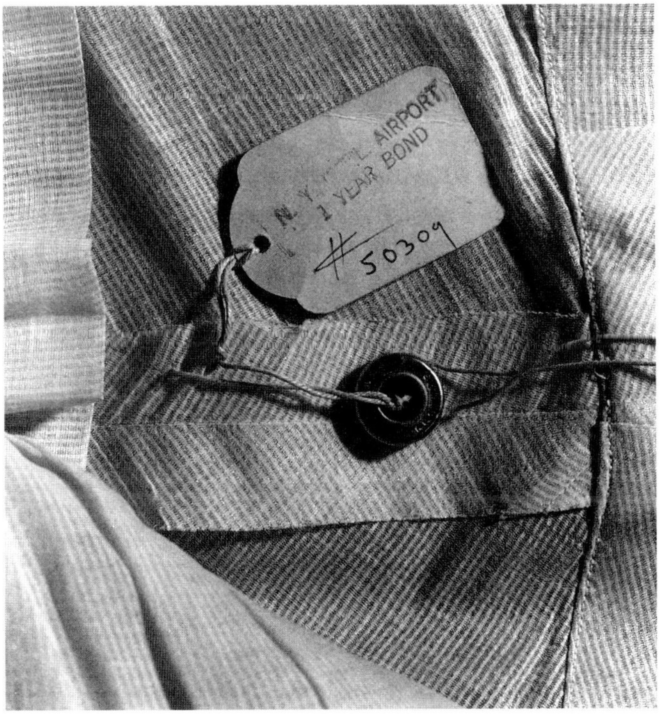

(b)

Figure 4a, b
Bond tag and seal located on the inside of the Hartnell petticoat. ROM. 970.286.ab (Photography Brian Boyle)

References

Barthes, Roland. 1983. *The Fashion System*, trans. Matthew Ward and Richard Howard. Toronto: McGraw-Hill Ryerson.

Beaudoin Ross, Jacqueline and Pamela Blackstock. 1991. "Costume in Canada: The Sequel." *Material History Review* 34 (fall): 42–67.

Breward, Christopher. 1995. *The Culture of Fashion*. Manchester and New York: Manchester University Press.

Coleman, Elizabeth Ann. 1989. *The Opulent Era. Fashions of Worth, Doucet and Pingat*. London: The Brooklyn Museum in Association with Thames and Hudson Ltd.

——, 1990. "Pourvu que vos robes vous aillent.' Quand les Américaines s'habillaient à Paris." In *Femmes fin de siècle 1885–1895*, pp. 133–43. Paris: Palais Galleria.

Cunningham, Patricia. 1988. "Beyond Artifacts and Object Chronology." *Dress* 14: 76–9.

Evans, Caroline and Minna Thornton. 1989. *Women and Fashion. A New Look*. London: Quartet Books.

Fields, Jill. 1997. Unpublished thesis. "The Production of Glamour: A Social History of Lingerie, 1909–1952." University of Southern California. (Thesis was not yet submitted at the time of writing this article).

Finkelstein, Joanne. 1996. *After A Fashion*. Melbourne: Melbourne University Press.

Guillaume, Valérie. 1993. *Jacques Fath*. Paris: Editions Paris Musées.

Harte, N. B. 1991. Foreword to *Textile History* 22, no. 2 (autumn): 150.

Harvey, John. 1995. *Men in Black*. Chicago: University of Chicago Press.

Hood, Adrienne. 1990. "Material Culture and Textiles: An Overview." *Material History Bulletin* 31 (spring): 5–10.

Lemire, Beverly. 1990. "Reflections on the Character of Consumerism, Popular Fashion and the English Market in the Eighteenth Century," *Material History Bulletin* 31 (spring): 65–70.

——, 1991. *Fashion's Favourite: The Cotton Trade and the Consumer in Britain, 1660–1800*. Pasold Research Fund: Oxford University Press.

——, 1994. "Re-dressing the History of Clothing: Guilds, Women, Workers and Ready-made Trade in England 1600–1800." Paper presented at the Costume Society of America Annual Meeting, Montreal.

Leventon, Melissa. 1989. "Shopping for Style: Couture in America," in *New Look to Now. French Haute Couture 1947–1987*, ed. Stephen de Petri and Melissa Leventon. New York: Rizzoli: 23–8.

Lipovetsky, Gilles. 1994. *The Empire of Fashion: Dressing Modern Democracy*. Trans. Catherine Porter. Princeton: Princeton University Press.

Miller, Daniel. 1987. *Material Culture*. Oxford: Basil Blackwell.

Miller, Lesley. 1993. *Cristóbal Balenciaga*. London: B.T. Batsford.

Parker, Rozsika. 1989. *The Subversive Stitch. Embroidery and the Making of the Feminine*. London: Routledge.

Rexford, Nancy. 1988. "Studying Garments for Their Own Sake: Mapping the World of Costume Scholarship." *Dress* 14: 68–75.

Roche, Daniel. 1989. *La culture des apparences. Une histoire du vêtement XVII–XVIII siècle*. Paris: Fayard.

Severa, Joan and Merrill Horswill. (1989). "Costume as Material Culture." *Dress* 15: 51–64.

Sonenscher, Michael. 1987. *Hatters of 18th Century France*. Berkeley and Los Angeles: University of California Press.

Steele, Valerie. 1985. *Fashion and Eroticism. Ideals of Feminine Beauty from the Victorian Era to the Jazz Age*. Oxford and London: Oxford University Press.

——, 1988. *Paris Fashion: A Cultural History*. New York and Oxford: Oxford University Press.

——, 1991. *Women of Fashion. Twentieth Century Designers*. New York: Rizzoli.

——, 1996. *Fetish: Fashion, Sex and Power*. New York: Oxford University Press.

Styles, John. 1993. "Manufacturing, Consumption and Design in Eighteenth-Century England," in *Consumption and the World of Goods*, ed. John Brewer and Roy Porter. London: Routledge.

Taylor, Lou. 1992. "Paris Couture 1940–1944," in *Chic Thrills. A Fashion Reader*, ed. Juliet Ash and Elizabeth Wilson. London: Pandora.

Thirsk, Joan. 1990. "Popular Consumption and the Mass Market in the Sixteenth to Eighteenth Centuries." *Material History Bulletin* 319 (spring): 51–8.

Ulrich, Laurel Thatcher. 1991. "Cloth, Clothing and Early American Social History." *Dress* 18: 39–48.

Veillon, Dominique. 1990. *La Mode sous l'Occupation: débrouillardise et coquetterie dans la France en guerre (1939–1945)*. Paris: Payot.

Weatherill, Lorna. 1988. *Consumer Behaviour and Material Culture in England, 1660–1760*. London: Routledge.

Wilson, Elizabeth. 1985. *Adorned in Dreams: Fashion and Modernity*. London: Virago Press.

Fashion Theory, Volume 1, Issue 3, pp.313–320
Reprints available directly from the Publishers.
Photocopying permitted by licence only.

Exhibition Review: Tanks and Trousseaus: Fashion in the Theater of War—*Forties Fashion and the New Look.* Imperial War Museum, London

Reviewed by Christopher Breward

February 12 – August 31, 1997

Entering under the lofty dome of the Imperial War Museum, London, between twin missile launchers aimed across the river towards the Palace of Westminster, the visitor to "Forties Fashion," a substantial temporary exhibition celebrating the fiftieth anniversary of Christian Dior's New Look, has first to negotiate a route through the debris of twentieth-century military history. The metal hulks of tanks, submarines and land periscopes appear to advance from all sides whilst Zeppelin observation cabins and Spitfires swoop from above, the atmosphere subtly impregnated with the fragrance of engine oil and rusting rivets. If one ever needed reminding that the re-experience of the past is a deeply gendered one then the gaggles of open-mouthed little boys and their

equally excited fathers, who caress, sketch and generally re-animate these steel and canvas hulks from former conflicts, impress the notion that war and its technology provide a strangely comforting cushion for the masculine ego. Despite its unequivocal name and awe-inspiring central gallery, The Imperial War Museum has done much to dispel the vision of battle as a great male adventure. Previous exhibitions centering on experience at the home front, together with moving permanent displays that emphasize the political and social cost of war for civilians and the active forces, do much to temper a nagging suspicion that the collection is a grand excuse for phallic triumphalism. As preparation for a show of dresses that hung from the backs of Hollywood goddesses, Utility suits and Parisian couture, however, even the "Blitz Experience" with its bangs and rumbles, its "roll out the barrel" blend of matriarchal defiance, provides but a pale premonition. To step purposely from fusillades to frocks feels like a bizarrely subversive and refreshing act.

As much as the paraphernalia of military engagement exerts an almost visceral and entirely romantic hold on its boyish admirers, the opening display stand of "Forties Fashion" draws an equally besotted, but very different audience under its spell, one which the Imperial War Museum is presumably more used to accommodating in its cinematheque reruns of black-and-white melodramas, or the more reflective spaces of its painting galleries. Here though, in the dark heart of the building, beneath a surreal glinting glass chandelier that once hung in Norman Hartnell's Bruton Street Couture House, stands a collection of black, white and silver evening gowns from Chanel and Molyneux, their sinuous contours dramatically lit; one, we are informed by the minimal labelling, worn by Garbo. Across the passageway James Gunn's image of pre-war Piccadilly hauteur, "Pauline Waiting," a frighteningly perfect combination of ocelot, black silk net and red finger-nails, stares covetously from the canvas at the set piece. Between the portrait and the mannequins, the curators have their audience suitably transfixed, for this is undoubtedly an exhibition that prioritizes the visual and the sensual over the cerebral. Here fashion exists as camp fantasy, thrown into sharper relief through its juxtaposition with the equally mannered escapism of war comics and campaign heroes in the galleries outside. I recall a London drag act whose catch-phrase was "Jungle Red," accompanied by a manic waving of the fingers. This, for the benefit of the uninitiated, was a reference to the modish shade of nail varnish flaunted by the shopping-crazed heroines of Cukor's cult 1939 classic "The Women," a film which runs as a leitmotif through "Forties Fashion and the New Look." That I should be reminded of the masquerade of gay theater in the midst of an exhibition purporting to set the introduction of the New Look in 1947 in its immediate historical and cultural context, one presumably marked by wartime deprivations flanked before and after by austerity, at first took me by surprise. By the end of the show (and a "show" in its true sense is what this exhibition turns out to be), an ongoing, indeed

Figure 1
Sir Hardy Amies design, 1947–9.

exhausting, rhetoric of spectacle and theatrical flourish left me wondering whether the Imperial War Museum had become the latest convert to Queer polemics!

This playfulness is all very well, and there is much scope within fashion studies for an examination of the ways in which sexuality and gender inform relationships with clothing and its representation or performance. The Imperial War Museum, it might be argued, provides an ideal setting for the playing out of those complex positions, and any attempt to overcome the usual depressing association of displayed historical clothing with the possessions of the deceased or an absence of life should be lauded. Ultimately, though, what should have been an enlightening by-product of the exhibition visitor's experience becomes here an overwhelming impression. Sensual gratification threatens to overshadow the fundamental debates thrown up by the selection of specific items from a particular period that has been isolated by fashion historians as a pivotal moment in the development of twentieth-century clothing. In other words, the splendor of the display elicits a very immediate response from the viewer, usually attached to memories of similar garments or textures, or underpinned by a strong sense of identification —the desire to possess the luxury on show. However, as a consistent narrative, linking garments together and making sense of the shift from 1930s bias-cut glamour to boxy wartime severity through to voluptuous 1950s escapism, or testing that narrative against the experiences of consumers at the time, the exhibition largely fails. Everything is in the right order, and the astute observer can trace the way that hemlines rise and fall; but it is far more difficult to gain any sense of the way such change is informed by factors lying outside the remit of Bond Street designers, Hollywood directors and style leaders. Economics, politics, class, markets, the whole range of influences dictating the production and consumption of clothing don't seem to impinge on the fantasy. Some of the blame lies with the exhibition texts. As stated, labels provide too brief a reference to date, designer and owner. Curators I know subscribe to the theory that museum visitors don't read; but these are the shortest I've ever seen and simply add to the impression that fashion is a subject for the frivolous: the tanks get more lines than this! Laminated binders containing reproductions of magazine and department store advertisements and other ephemeral items are placed strategically throughout the displays, presumably to provide contextual information. The images are, however, left largely to speak for themselves, and the constant clicking of the pages provides percussion to the soundtrack of popular 1940s songs played through the intercom. The fashion journalist Colin McDowell has written an accompanying souvenir book, which sparkles in the same manner as the exhibition with anecdotes and wonderful illustrations. But there is a lack of references and no bibliography, and its celebratory tone will frustrate the historian who needs to know about the provenance of the items or their relevant interpretative sources.

Figure 2
Sir Hardy Amies design, 1947–9.
© Imperial War Museum

So, the remit of "Forties Fashion and the New Look" is not perhaps an academic one, and it may be unfair to criticize it on those grounds. The poster advertising its run on the London Underground has the ballet dancer Darcey Bussell posing in Dior's iconic "Bar" suit amidst crumbling Corinthian pillars, like a fairy cavorting amidst the crumbs of a wedding cake. Photographed recently by Snowdon, it makes direct reference to the photographic methods of his earlier career and increases the sensation of confection that the exhibition encourages. Its mischievous re-interpretation of the historical record should have prepared me for an exhibition high on drama, but low on interpretation. At the same time, though, its constructed inauthenticity does hint at the pleasures of viewing in store, the delicious ironies thrown up by letting the exhibits expose their own associations (with the undoubted aid of atmospheric sound track, moody lighting, back projections and film clips). Bussell, often presented in the media as the feisty face of classical dance in the 1990s, unwittingly teeters in an outfit that has variously been dismissed by commentators and historians as the incarnation of women's entrapment in those retrogressive models of femininity encouraged by the post-war status quo as a means of negating any influence achieved during wartime, or lauded as an embodiment of the elegance and escapism that constitute women's entry to emotional and erotic other lives, fashion as empowerment. These are not themes deliberately followed through in the exhibition, but they are manifested subliminally through its design and selection of objects. Potential Bussell fans, the old ladies and little girls who throng to Covent Garden Ballet matinées, packed the galleries when I was there, with a few male couples thrown in for good measure. Their comments on the exhibits proved more enlightening than the official labels with respect to the varied hidden meanings attached to those garments which defined the feminine between 1930 and 1950. Studying Horst's much parodied, but yearning 1939 image of a Mainbocher corset, one woman, a master of bathos, whispered to her companion that "my nan had some of those pink things." Nostalgia, perhaps, is the primary sensation encouraged by a display that prioritizes notions of the "classic" image or the "classic" cut, and many visitors appeared to be pining romantically for the lost era of glamor and sophistication conjured up by the exhibition designers. Nostalgia, though, is a dangerously distorting mirror through which to view the past.

For pure theater "Forties Fashion and the New Look" is well worth the admission price. Its highlights, for those who crave instant fashion gratification, include the wonderful juxtaposition of a John Lewis wedding suit in burgundy velvet with fur muff worn in October 1939 by one Constance Creswell (we are not told who she was) and Winston Churchill's red velvet siren suit. "Materials," we are informed by adjacent text panels, "were in short supply" and "practicality became the order of the day." I'm not convinced that plush velvets constituted

practicality, but their absurdity in this context raised a smile. Two telephones provide oral testimonies of wartime experiences, and through the directness of the spoken word I came closest to understanding the way that women's relationship to fashion between 1939 and 1945 was both a bonding forum for camaraderie and a terrain riven through with class distinctions. Hearing the cut-glass diction of a *Woman's Own* editor appraising Utility fashions and the broad northern lilt of a Hull factory worker's recollection of the sharing of clothing coupons was like comparing Celia Johnson with Gracie Fields. Textiles printed with patriotic or propaganda images and slogans are particularly striking: a voluminous crimson dressing-gown emblazoned with the Shakespearian tag "this sceptred isle" offers one example of home-front bravado and a neat (though unexplored) link through to English post-war obsessions with the decorative and traditional, epitomized by neo-romantic painting or Minton's wistful illustrations for Elizabeth David cookbooks. A pair of 1944 darned socks from Holland reminds one briefly of the grimmer realities. Turning into a bunker-like tunnel of painted brick and corrugated iron, a line of mannequins in uniform throws another perspective on war wear. Accompanied by a soundtrack of the barrack-room favorites "Home on leave" and "The thingamy bob girl," the effect seems closer to a Noel Coward naval revue than the Battle of Britain, particularly when it becomes apparent that all this khaki was designed by Digby Morton and Hardy Amies, or available at Lillywhites and Austin Reed if designer labels were beyond your pocket.

The pervading rhetoric of gentlemanly reserve and stiff upper lips contrasts beautifully with the adjacent "glamour" passage. Framed in ornate "surrealist" borders, boutique windows open up on to scenes of escapist Hollywood luxury. A particular favorite with the Bussell fans must be a huge dressing table loaded with as much Max Factor and Estée Lauder as a girl could need. Extravagant Adrian confections for Joan Crawford, Lucille Ball, Ginger Rogers and Claudette Colbert flank a video projection of the color fashion-show scene from "The Women." The functional, modernist settings for Utility wear provide a more prosaic link through to the fairy tale fantasy of the "Theatre de la Mode", crowned by Cocteau's scene of swooping miniature mannequins "I married a witch," which itself pre-empts the supposed romanticism of the New Look proper.

The final gallery, with its stiff formality, mannequins frozen in yards of skirting and severe boned jackets, struck me as disappointing after all the build-up. A photograph of middle-class women in their moth-eaten furs protesting against further clothing rationing in a Bayswater street of 1946 certainly communicates the popular desire for something clean and new, a release from wartime stringency, and I overheard one older visitor admiring the very timely "Cherie" blue silk taffeta dress by Dior say to her companion "Do you remember? It was so exciting, the prettiest clothes I've ever worn." Indeed, the sharp lines and elegant

proportions of the New Look did represent a radical departure in 1947, but their impact here is watered down by all the effort directed towards presenting the imaginative choices of the war years as anything but dull and restrictive. After Ferragamo's 1942 multicolored platform shoe and McClelland Barclay's fizzing portrait of the flame headed Anna Neagle in gold lamé, the restrained ivory silk and black crêpe of Dior's Bar suit appear rather muted. I'm not sure if this was the Imperial War Museum's intention, but in prioritizing visual effect over a communication of context or a more overt attempt at interpretation, the visitor is left to draw his or her own comparisons and judgements. Without a doubt, I enjoyed this exhibition for its humor and spectacle. What worried me was its resistance to any broader engagement with recent scholarly work on clothing in the period. Peter McNeil, Angela Partington and Lou Taylor, amongst others, have all offered finely nuanced and helpful studies of fashion in this period in the context of design history and Barbara Burman has orchestrated an influential project on the meanings attached to home sewing at Winchester School of Art, but as far as I could tell their influence was largely ignored here. The juxtaposition of lipstick and khaki at the Imperial War Museum is both shocking and fun. Its deeper repercussions are left for others to unravel.

Fashion Theory, Volume 1, Issue 3, pp.321–328
Reprints available directly from the Publishers.
Photocopying permitted by licence only.

Exhibition Review: *Art/Fashion*. Guggenheim Museum SoHo

Reviewed by
Ena Szkoda

March 12 – June 8, 1997

Art/Fashion was organized in cooperation with the Guggenheim Museum as a component of the 1996 Biennale di Firenze. Last fall, the Florence Biennial presented *Il tempo e le moda* (Looking at Fashion), a series of exhibitions dedicated to the exploration of the connection between art and fashion. With *Art/Fashion,* curators Germano Celant, Luigi Settembrini, and Ingrid Sischy, have brought the Biennale di Firenze to the Guggenheim Museum SoHo where an extended version of the original Italian exhibit is on view from March 12 through June 8, 1997. The three-part exhibition is also accompanied by a fully-illustrated catalog published by Skira.

Art/Fashion begins with a broad historical survey of artists who have collaborated with fashion designers or incorporated fashion-related

issues in their work. The second segment presents the works of eight contemporary artists who use fashion to express a range of issues including body, gender and sexuality. The final section documents the 1996 Florence Biennale with a photographic display of collaborative installations by pairs of fashion designers and artists. The Guggenheim mounted these photos in structures meant to recall the pavilions that housed the installations in Florence during the Biennale.

The exhibition opens with the work of the Italian Futurists. The Futurist costumes presented in *Art/Fashion* are loud, boldly colored, and strikingly modern in appearance, such as the Fortunato Depero-designed vest with a graphic pattern of stylized blue fish. Also on display was Giacomo Balla's "Futurist Manifesto of Men's Clothing," which encouraged men to use clothing as not only a way to "reconstruct the universe" but to "spread good humor" as well. Like the Futurists, some Russian Constructivists turned to the design of costume and textiles as part of their project to produce utilitarian and proletarian art that was "socially and consciously useful . . . [and] bound indissolubly with life" (Arvatov 1976). Although the art of the Russian avant-garde is undeniably powerful, the inclusion of these objects is problematic in as much as Constructivist artists such as Liubov Popova and Varvara Stepanova publicly condemned the very idea of fashion as outdated and bourgeois. The inclusion of three reconstructed garments was also surprising, because dress (either original or reconstructed) was conspicuously missing from the Guggenheim's exhaustive exhibition in 1992 on the art of the Russian Avant-Garde.

The next room was dedicated mostly to the work of Sonia Delaunay and Elsa Schiaparelli. Although the smallest room in the exhibition, it presented the most successful representation of a merger between art and fashion. In the clothes and textiles that she designed, Delaunay used pattern, texture and color to express Simultaneity, a type of Orphic Cubism that supposedly entranced or transported the viewer to a point beyond linear time and space. Works by Delaunay exhibited in *Art/Fashion* include not only many textile and clothing designs but a handful of actual costumes as well. The exhibition provided a rare opportunity to view garments by Delaunay, and the method the Guggenheim used to mount the costumes was also of interest: an "invisible" mannequin or form was custom-made for each garment and suspended from the ceiling, allowing the viewer an immediate and physical connection to the "absent" human form. The "invisible" mannequins also added another dimension to the sensual, Surrealist-inspired designs of Elsa Schiaparelli. Although an artist in her own right, Schiaparelli is more famous for having recruited famous Surrealist artists, such as Salvador Dali and Jean Cocteau, to collaborate on embroidery, textile and advertising designs. Among the extraordinary examples of her work presented in *Art/Fashion* is the Schiaparelli/Dali "tear" dress. Dali designed the textile from which her dress was made: a trompe l'oeil effect

of rips and tears. Later Dali incorporated her dress design in his painting "Three Young Surrealist Women Holding in Their Arms the Skins of an Orchestra."

Between two larger galleries was a transitional space where photographs from the 1930s and 1940s were displayed, such as the arty fashion photos of Georges Platt Lynes and the fashion-infused art of Man Ray. Unfortunately, at this point, not only does the pace of the exhibition speed up, but the overall cohesion of *Art/Fashion* begins to unravel.

The photographs led into a large, open room devoted almost entirely to Italian abstract artists of the 1960s. Although examples included two collaborations between the Op-artist, Getulio Alvani, and the fashion designer, Germana Marucelli, the unfortunate presentation generated little visual interest. Three rows of anonymous and bodiless garments swayed in the breeze created by museum-goers. Fifteen feet to the right were the uninformative (and slightly confusing) labels for these objects. Lucio Fontana was the best represented artist in the room, with three canvases and five garments. The artist took a formal element from his slashed canvases and translated the concept into the vernacular of clothing as V-necks, deep pleats, and provocative cutaways. For some reason, next to three Fontana dresses, the Guggenheim placed a reconstruction of an awkward, color-block dress by Ellsworth Kelly.

The following three rooms included art from the 1960s, 1970s and 1980s, with examples ranging from Performance and Conceptual art to Pop and Deconstructivism. Pieces by Niki de Saint Phalle, Christo and Arman comment more on the fashionable attitudes of their day than on any connection to the fashion of the times. One of Joseph Beuys' felt suits aroused suspicion that the Guggenheim had abruptly altered its meaning of the word "fashion." Until this time, *Art/Fashion* had attempted "to explore the frequent and fertile interaction between art and fashion." But at this point, the art ceased to explore any such interactions and became a one-sided presentation of the various ways artists view fashion.

Although it was not obvious at first where the second part of *Art/Fashion* began, the exhibition lived up to its promise to present contemporary art which "employ[ed] a vocabulary associated with fashion to investigate sensitive current issues relating to the body, gender, identity and representation." None of this work represented a direct collaboration with a fashion or textile designer, although some art did appear to have been directly influenced by current themes in fashion. Three pieces by Rosemarie Trockel were shown: a two-necked turtleneck sweater, a dress with a woolmark symbol over each breast, and a patterned textile stretched on the wall like a canvas. Judith Shea's work is described as bringing feminine issues to minimalism, but her references to pattern pieces seemed superficial. Wiebke Siem's orderly presentation of 12 felt hats and nine wooden shoes looked like the toys of an anal-

retentive child. Jana Sterbak explored gender issues in pieces such as, "Nightdress," a sheer nightgown with attached chest hair, and "I want you to feel the way I feel," an electrified wire dress. "Absorption," a photographic documentation of what appeared to be a human-sized molting worm, was a cute reference to Beuys' wool felt suit.

Charles Le Dray's intentionally precious installation included actual items of clothing. "Animal Act," a handsewn velvet "elephant" suit with buttons for eyes and a pants leg stuffed and hung sideways as a sort of elephant trunk/penis, is both adorable and subversively sexual. Along the edge of the floor is another piece by Le Dray, entitled "workwork-workworkwork." At first glance, the handmade, doll-sized clothes and magazines simply appear quaint, but closer examination reveals that some garments are soiled and some magazines have provocative titles, such as "Trapped By Greed." The two Mylar sculptures by Oliver Herring were less clearly connected to fashion. The sheet of silver Mylar that stretched across the wall as a large painting, was knitted: was that the connection? Was the seated sculpture somehow commenting on the human body?

The rivers of sumptuous fabric in Beverly Semmes' "Pink Arms" were overwhelmingly seductive. Her oversized dress of blue organza flowed down the wall and across the floor to the viewers' feet with the pink arms of the dress, in almost blood-like fuchsia velvet, pooling at the center. This was a powerful and aesthetically successful piece. Even more powerful was Jan Fabre's "Wall of Descending Angels," a dress formed entirely out of scarabs on iron net, which was simultaneously repulsive and sensuous. Even the eerie shadow on the wall, echoing the curvy lines of the dress, was beautiful. More shocking was "Messenger," a similar dress of scarabs turned, almost sacrilegiously, upside down and ripped open to reveal an empty cavity. Were the entrails eaten or simply nonexistent? The eye is drawn to the beauty of the individual insects recalling, for this reviewer, Schiaparelli's suit with scarab buttons in the collection of the Metropolitan Museum of Art's Costume Institute.

In the last room were miniature pavilions which represented actual pavilions in Florence. Each structure contained a documentary photograph of an installation jointly created by a fashion designer and a fine artist. While the structures were interesting, it was difficult to judge the collaborative installations from a two-dimensional photograph. For example, the photograph of the room by Julian Schnabel and Azzedine Alaïa did not appear to present a collaboration but a competition where each artist completed his part of the room separately. Occasionally, one artist's vision seemed to supersede that of the other. For instance, the Jenny Holzer/Helmut Lang piece, a completely black room with a central column of LED-displays, appeared to rely heavily on Holzer's artistic style. Some artist/designer pairings seemed odd. Why was aging pop artist Roy Lichtenstein paired with Gianni Versace, a fashion designer known for his outrageous styles? This pairing was one of the more

Figure 1
Getulio Alviani for Germana Marucelli. *Positive Negative* 1964. Black and white jersey. Collection of the artist, Milan. Reproduced with kind permission of the Guggenheim Museum

Heilinger & Co

successful, however, as the duo stuck to basic colors (red, white, yellow and blue) and simple black shapes, dots and lines. Also among these installations is the most successful Oliver Herring piece in the show: sheets of knitted Mylar encased identical pieces of clothing by Rei Kawakubo, which were laid out on a long table, like candy, pills or sterilized equipment in a pristine environment.

Although it is admirable that the Guggenheim's curators would not commit to any one definition of the word fashion, the decision adversely affected the thematic cohesion of *Art/Fashion*. Additionally, the inclusion of the documentary photographs in the last room of the exhibition helped only to create confusion. Apparently many artists and fashion designers are currently in collaboration. Why was this not explored in the second segment? *Art/Fashion* furthers the discussion of art and fashion, but there is still a need for other more fully developed exhibitions.

References

Arvatov Boris. 1976. "The Proletariat and Leftist Art, 1922" in *Russian Art of the Avant-Garde: Theories and Criticism, 1920–1934*, John E. Bowlt. ed. and translator. New York: Viking Press, 1976.

Figure 2
Joseph Beuys. *Felt Suit*. 1970. Felt Collection & Bruno and Antonella Pisaturo, Naples, Italy. Reproduced with kind permission of the Guggenheim Museum

Fashion Theory, Volume 1, Issue 3, pp.329–332
Reprints available directly from the Publishers.
Photocopying permitted by licence only.

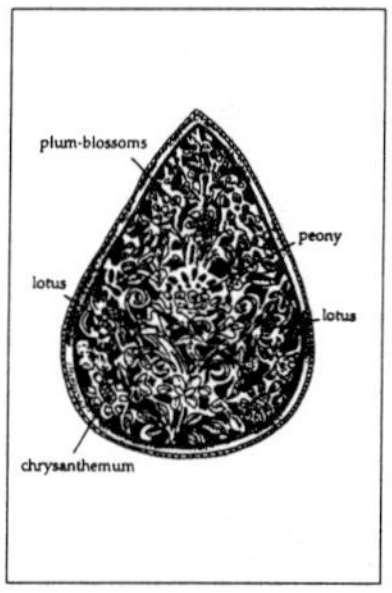

Exhibition Review: *Adornment for Eternity: Status and Rank in Chinese Ornament*. The China Institute In America, New York

Reviewed by John S. Major

February 6 – June 28, 1997

John S. Major, a specialist in early Chinese intellectual history, lives in New York. He is the author of *Heaven and Earth in Early Han Thought* (SUNY Press, 1993).

For many years the China Institute in America has been famous for using its small, attractive galleries to present exhibitions distinguished by specialized but well-focused subjects, superbly chosen objects, and a high level of connoisseurship designed to appeal to the Institute's core audience of collectors and serious amateurs of Chinese art. Exhibitions there from years past—of Neolithic jades, of Yixing ceramic teapots, of traditional Chinese art glass, to name just a few highlights—remain bright in my memory as examples of how small galleries can sometimes present exhibitions that larger institutions cannot match for taste, intelligence, and a gem-like quality of being just right. It is therefore all the more distressing to have to report that "Adornment for Eternity" is

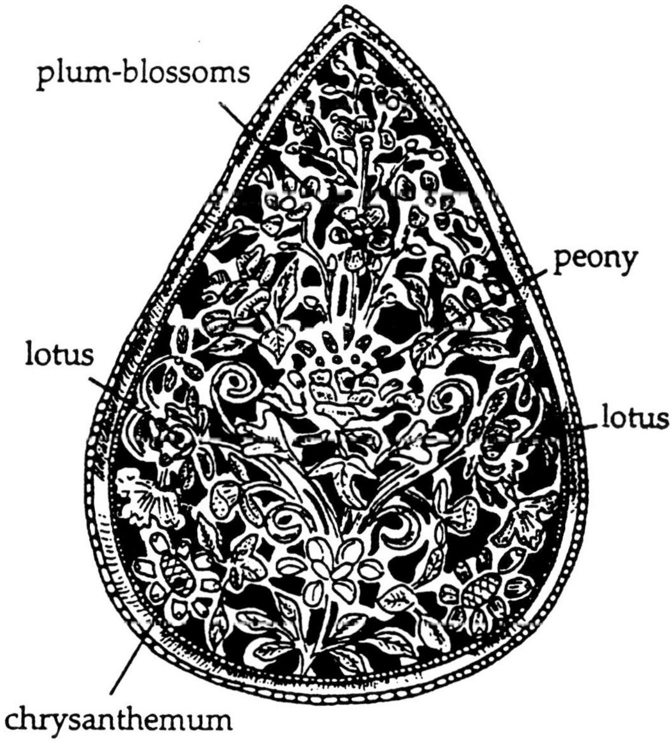

Figure 1
Drawing of an openwork gold scent-container from the Song Dynasty, from the gallery guide to "Adornment for Eternity" at the China Institute in America, New York.

far below the China Institute's normal level of achievement. It is, in fact, a deeply disappointing exhibition; this review will be largely an account of its missed opportunities.

"Adornment for Eternity" is a joint undertaking of the China Institute and the Denver Art Museum, where the exhibition previously appeared. All the items on display are on long-term loan to the Denver Art Museum from the Mengdiexuan Foundation. The exhibition consists of a hundred or so small decorative items, mostly of metal, mostly (but not all) intended to be worn or carried about the person. The objects, though of high quality, are unexceptional in the aggregate: one finds here the usual sash-hooks, hairpins, plaques, earrings, and belt-ornaments. Bronze mirrors are a somewhat puzzling addition to the mixture; interesting and often beautiful though they are, they were normally kept on wooden stands, or put away in brocade-covered boxes, and though they must have been carried about from time to time, they are not normally part of the "adornment" of traditional Chinese costume. The objects range in era from the Shang through the Ming, and they are too discontinuous to impart much useful historical information about this span of almost 3,000 years.

The exhibition's title implies that the objects on display were tomb goods, designed to adorn for all eternity the person with whom they were buried; but the viewer is given no information about the graves in which the objects were found, if indeed the inference that these are grave goods is correct. Nor is any substantial information provided about how these things formed part of an ensemble, how (if at all) they fit into patterns of fashionable behavior, or about how (despite the exhibition's subtitle) these objects indicate anything about status and rank (nor, needless to say, about gender, age, or other categories of social distinction). The bare objects are displayed in cases in a way that gives no sense of how they might have adorned an actual person; three reproductions of details from scroll paintings give the only visual guidance to how some of the objects might have been worn in real life. One of the few interesting bits of actual information presented about the objects concerns the replacement of sash-hooks by belts (adorned with metal plaques and pendants) in the first century AD, a change supposedly spurred by changes in the sumptuary laws.

More generally, the little information that is provided for the exhibition-goer, in the form of a photocopied handout and a few wall-mounted descriptive statements, emphasizes the décor of the objects themselves, and the metallurgical or other techniques employed in making them, rather than their significance as part of a system of clothing and adornment. Here, in its entirety, is one descriptive statement, on "Earrings and Hairpins":

> Initially both men and women wore hairpins. As practical tools hairpins held long loose hair close to the head and out of the eyes. The simple straight pins, however, evolved into elaborate crown-like diadems worn by women. Combs were both worn in the hair and used to comb the hair.
>
> Earrings belong to the realm of pure adornment and have no practical use. They emphasize the beauty and indicate the status of the wearer.

Of the many things wrong with this statement, let us look at just a few. First, notice the hostility to the very idea of adornment, betrayed first in the assumption that it was fine for both men and women to wear hairpins when they were "practical," but that when they became "elaborate" they were (presumably appropriately) worn only by women; this hostility is made explicit in the statement that earrings "emphasize the beauty . . . of the wearer" and "have no practical use." Next one might consider the odd notion that there was nothing practical about a device to "indicate the status of [a] wearer" (though, of course, we are asked to take this function on faith, being told nothing about how earrings actually performed that function); surely a semiotics of status is eminently practical in a hierarchical society. There is, too, a false

historicism at work here, in the idea that hairpins "evolved" (as if they were little Darwinian animals) from "practical" straight pins to more elaborate and decorative ones—not a word about changing styles of adornment, the introduction (e.g. from non-Chinese cultures) of new motifs and designs, changing technology in the manufacture of decorative items, a general increase in social wealth and conspicuous consumption, or indeed anything that would qualify as interpretation; we are left with a simple, prim statement of decline from archaic simplicity and practicality to later ornamentation and excess (one is left to wonder what might be meant by "initially"). Along the way we are treated, too, to a stunning error of fact, for these hairpins were never used by the Chinese to keep "loose hair close to the head and out of the eyes." In fact, the Chinese regarded it as essential to civilized behavior to wear one's hair in a bun or topknot, into which hairpins might be inserted; Chinese visitors to frontier regions never tired of exclaiming in affected horror about how the "barbarians" wore their hair unbound.

One could go on, but why belabor the case? This exhibition perhaps succeeds on its own terms as a display of high-quality small decorative items, but it has nothing at all to say about adornment, status, rank, or eternity. For anyone interested in fashion and self-fashioning as social and cultural phenomena, the message of this *mélange* of misinformation and missed opportunities is that much work remains to be done to convince the museum and art-historical worlds that these are subjects to be taken seriously.

Fashion Theory, Volume 1, Issue 3, pp.333–336
Reprints available directly from the Publishers.

Reviewed by Susan North

Book Review

The Politics of Women's Work: The Paris Garment Trades, 1750–1915, Judith G. Coffin, Princeton University Press, 1996

289 pp, 22 illustrations, bibliography, index

As the title indicates, this is a book about labor history. It does not concern itself with the history or the culture of fashion, but with the industries that produced them. In particular, the author relates how the garment industries became associated with women and subsequently

how ideas of gender appropriateness developed to justify what had become "women's work". Nevertheless, *The Politics of Women's Work* is essential reading, not only for students of social history and women's studies, but also for the dress historian.

Judith Coffin is a labor historian and writes primarily to challenge several myths associated with the garment trades and theories about the development of these trades after the Industrial Revolution. The first is the idea that sewing and the garment industries were traditionally the preserve of women. As most dress historians know, the tailoring guild was always a strictly male preserve and so was that of the ready- made merchants which arose in the eighteenth century. The documentation accompanying the confrontations between the tailors and the women's guilds (linen drapers and seamstresses) reveals the perceived rights and expectations of each group. In a society which provided few economic opportunities for women, the right to sew was crucial for those who had to support themselves and their families. The exclusiveness of the female guilds was seen by women as the only means to protect themselves from exploitation – economic and sexual – by men.

The second myth that Coffin disputes is one held dear by social and labor historians: that after the Industrial Revolution, the amount of work done in the home (termed "homework" by the author) declined, as more and more industries were organized on the factory model, due to increased use of machinery. The author demonstrates very clearly that in the case of the garment trades this did not happen. In fact, "homework" increased throughout the nineteenth century, as manufacturers sought to reduce labor and production costs, and to avoid newly introduced laws concerning working hours and conditions. The new technology of the sewing machine was seen as an aid to homeworkers, allowing them a more rapid means of production. Although the sewing machine was originally intended for use by military tailors, by the 1860s manufacturers were concentrating on producing models suitable for the home, and retailers soon established the means by which these expensive machines could be hired or purchased by working-class women. As the author's research illustrates, the majority of married women preferred to work at home. It gave them some control over their rate of production, it allowed them to combine their waged labor with their (unwaged) house work and child care, and it freed them from the perceived dangers of factory work, including sexual harassment.

As well as outlining these changes in the garment trades, Coffin also investigates the moral attitudes which developed to justify them. The late eighteenth century had already established the attitude that women were imaginative, dextrous and fond of ornament (perfect attributes for the fashion trades), in contrast to the robust and inventive masculine nature. In the nineteenth century, social reformers continued the moral defence of women's work, particularly of "homework". Women were simply too delicate for the brutishness and physical dangers of factory

work. In reality, the primary motivation for employing women was financial; they could be paid less on the grounds that they were merely augmenting their husbands' wages.

It was not until the early twentieth century that social reformers uncovered the squalid truth about urban "homework": cramped quarters, sixteen-hour days and appallingly low pay. The hysteria over the possible spread of disease through "homework" was eagerly fanned by journalists. Radical reformers decried the oppression and abuse of homeworkers, while conservative critics worried about the declining birthrate and poor family life such conditions caused. Overriding all these concerns was the anxiety about France's competitiveness in the garment trade. In the campaign to secure the rights of women homeworkers, feminists were supported by doctors, social workers, health and housing experts and lawyers, yet there was no consensus on how the problem should be solved because these reformers came from both the radical and conservative ends of the political spectrum. Some felt that "homework" was the source of the problem: as long as women worked at home they would never organize into unions and would never benefit from legislation that controlled pay and working conditions in factories. Others felt that the issue was wages, not the location of work. If homeworkers were paid a decent wage, the argument ran, they would be relieved of the poverty that was the cause of the terrible conditions of "homework".

Although *The Politics of Women's Work* limits its range of study to France, Coffin makes interesting parallels with similar developments in Britain and the United States, particularly in area of union activity. Yet France's experience is unique for a variety of reasons, cultural and political. The neglect shown the women worker in France was a direct reflection of women's lowly social status in general. Because of the garment industry's association with women workers and products for women's consumption, neither government nor industrialists took seriously the problems and conditions of its workers, despite the fact that the clothing trades, particularly couture, were recognized as crucial to France's economic health.

Coffin's research draws upon an extremely wide range of primary sources, from eighteenth-century guild literature to a long series of government labor reports in the nineteenth and early twentieth centuries. Newspaper accounts, advertising, the reports from international industrial exhibitions, police documentation on strikes, literature on unions and feminist congresses have all been drawn upon in her research. Not only has the author a firm grasp on the textual sources, but she also makes good analyzes of the visual imagery in advertising posters. Covering such a vast amount of material requires much condensation, yet the author does not oversimplify. One of the merits of this work is the effort made to emphasize the complexity of garment labor at any given time. Coffin has a firm grip of the details and the exceptions, as

well as general trends. Another of the book's virtues is the author's clear and straightforward style; although the subject is complicated, its presentation is not.

It is sobering to note that many of the issues raised in *The Politics of Women's Work* are still relevant and distressing in the late twentieth-century garment industries. Immigrant women still labor in sweatshops in the East End of London for a pittance, and companies such as Nike and Mitre stand accused of making huge profits on the poorly paid workers of Asia, who sew at home and in oppressive factories. *The Politics of Women's Work* is an important and well researched contribution to labor, social and dress history, as well as a timely background study of issues about gender inequality and labor exploitation still pertinent today.

Susan North
Assistant Curator
Textiles & Dress
V&A Museum

Notes for Contributors

Articles should be approximately 25 pages in length and *must* include a three-sentence biography of the author(s). Interviews should not exceed 15 pages and do not require an author biography. Film, exhibition and book reviews are normally 500 to 1,000 words in length. The Publishers will require a disk as well as a hard copy of any contributions (please mark clearly on the disk what word-processing program has been used).

Fashion Theory: The Journal of Dress, Body & Culture will produce one issue a year devoted to a single topic. Persons wishing to organize a topical issue are invited to submit a proposal which contains a hundred-word description of the topic together with a list of potential contributors and paper subjects. Proposals are accepted only after review by the journal editor and in-house editorial staff at Berg Publishers.

Manuscripts

Manuscripts should be submitted to: *Fashion Theory: The Journal of Dress, Body & Culture*. Manuscripts will be acknowledged by the editor and entered into the review process discussed below. Manuscripts without illustrations will not be returned unless the author provides a self-addressed stamped envelope. Submission of a manuscript to the journal will be taken to imply that it is not being considered elsewhere for publication, and that if accepted for publication, it will not be published elsewhere, in the same form, in any language, without the consent of the editor and publisher. It is a condition of acceptance by the editor of a manuscript for publication that the publishers automatically acquire the copyright of the published article throughout the world. *Fashion Theory: The Journal of Dress, Body & Culture* does not pay authors for their manuscripts nor does it provide retyping, drawing, or mounting of illustrations.

Style

U.S. spelling and mechanicals are to be used. Authors are advised to consult *The Chicago Manual of Style (14th Edition)* as a guideline for style. *Webster's Dictionary* is our arbiter of spelling. We encourage the use of major subheadings and, where appropriate, second-level subheadings. Manuscripts submitted for consideration as an article must contain: a title page with the full title of the article, the author(s) name and address, and a three-sentence biography for each author. Do not place the author's name on any other page of the manuscript.

Manuscript Preparation

Manuscripts must be typed double-spaced (including quotations, notes, and references cited), one side only, with at least one-inch margins on standard paper using a typeface no smaller than 12pts. The original manuscript and a copy of the text on disk *(please ensure it is clearly marked with the word-processing program that has been used) must* be submitted, along with black and white *original* photographs (to be returned). Authors should retain a copy for their records. Any necessary artwork *must* be submitted with the manuscript.

Footnotes

Footnotes appear as 'Notes' at the end of articles. Authors are advised to include footnote material in the text whenever possible. Notes are to be numbered consecutively throughout the paper and are to be typed double-spaced at the end of the text. (Do not use any footnoting or end-noting programs which your software may offer as this text becomes irretrievably lost at the typesetting stage.)

References

The list of references should be limited to, and inclusive of, those publications actually cited in the text. References are to be cited in the body of the text in parentheses with author's last name, the year of original publication, and page number—e.g., (Rouch 1958: 45). Titles and publication information appear as 'References' at the end of the article and should be listed alphabetically by author and chronologically for each author. Names of journals and publications should appear in full. Film and video information appears as 'Filmography'. References cited should be typed double-spaced on a separate page. *References not presented in the style required will be returned to the author for revision.*

Tables

All tabular material should be part of a separately numbered series of 'Tables'. Each table must be typed on a separate sheet and identified by a short descriptive title. Footnotes for tables appear at the bottom of the table. Marginal notations on manuscripts should indicate approximately where tables are to appear.

Figures

All illustrative material (drawings, maps, diagrams, and photographs) should be designated 'Figures'. They must be submitted in a form suitable for publication without redrawing. Drawings should be carefully done with black ink on either hard, white, smooth-surfaced board or good quality tracing paper. Ordinarily, computer-generated drawings are not of publishable quality. Photographs should be black and white glossy prints (the publishers will not accept color) and should be numbered on the back to key with captions. Whenever possible, photographs should be 8 x 10 inches. All figures should be numbered consecutively. All captions should be typed double-spaced on a separate page. Marginal notations on manuscripts should indicate approximately where figures are to appear. While the editors and publishers will use ordinary care in protecting all figures submitted, they cannot assume responsibility for their loss or damage. Authors are discouraged from submitting rare or non-replaceable materials. It is the author's responsibility to secure written copyright clearance on *all* photographs and drawings that are not in the public domain.

Criteria for Evaluation

Fashion Theory: The Journal of Dress, Body & Culture is a refereed journal. Manuscripts will be accepted only after review by both the editors and anonymous reviewers deemed competent to make professional judgments concerning the quality of the manuscript. Upon request, authors will receive reviewers' evaluations.

Reprints for Authors

Twenty-five reprints of authors' articles will be provided to the first named author free of charge. Additional reprints may be purchased upon request.

Fashion Theory: The Journal of Dress, Body & Culture

Editor
Dr. Valerie Steele
The Museum at the Fashion Institute of Technology, E201
Seventh Avenue at 27th Street
New York, NY 10001-5992
USA
Fax: +1 212 924 3958
e-mail: steelemajor@earthlink.net

Aims and Scope

The importance of studying the body as a site for the deployment of discourses is well-established in a number of disciplines. By contrast, the study of fashion has, until recently, suffered from a lack of critical analysis. Increasingly, however, scholars have recognized the cultural significance of self-fashioning, including not only clothing but also such body alterations as tattooing and piercing. *Fashion Theory* takes as its starting point a definition of 'fashion' as the cultural construction of the embodied identity. It aims to provide an interdisciplinary forum for the rigorous analysis of cultural phenomena ranging from footbinding to fashion advertising.

Anyone wishing to submit an article, interview, or a book, film or exhibition review for possible publication in this journal should contact Valerie Steele (at the address listed below) or the Editorial Department at Berg (150 Cowley Road, Oxford, OX4 1JJ, UK; e-mail: enquiry@berg.demon.co.uk).

Notes for Contributors can be found at the back of the journal.

ISSN: 1362-704X

Editorial Board

Ordering Information — Four issues per volume. One volume per annum. 1997: Volume 1

By mail: Berg Publishers,
150 Cowley Road,
Oxford,
OX4 1JJ,
UK.

By fax: +44 (0) 1865 791165

By telephone: +44 (0) 1865 245104

By e-mail: enquiry@berg.demon.co.uk

Inquiries

Editorial: Kathryn Earle, Managing Editor, e-mail: kearle@berg1.demon.co.uk

Production: Sara Everett, e-mail: severett@berg.demon.co.uk

Advertising + subscriptions: Paul Millicheap, e-mail: pmillicheap@berg.demon.co.uk

Subscription Rates:

Institutional base list subscription price: £86.00, US$120.00.

Individuals' subscription price: £35.00, US$48.00.

Reprints of Individual Articles

Copies of individual articles may be obtained from the Publishers at the appropriate fees. Write to: Berg, 150 Cowley Road, Oxford, OX4 1JJ, UK.

Printed in the United Kingdom.
SEPTEMBER 1997

Issue 3 September 1997

Edited by Dr. Valerie Steele

Fashion Theory

The Journal of Dress, Body & Culture

BERG